ASHLEY ATWOOD

Travel to Phoenix, Arizona

A Guide and Journal for Activities, Restaurants and Daytrip Destinations for Vacationers and Traveling Professionals

SUNSHINE HILL
PROPERTIES

First published by Sunshine Hill Properties 2023

Copyright © 2023 by Ashley Atwood

All rights reserved. No part of this publication may be reproduced, stored or transmitted in any form or by any means, electronic, mechanical, photocopying, recording, scanning, or otherwise without written permission from the publisher. It is illegal to copy this book, post it to a website, or distribute it by any other means without permission.

Ashley Atwood asserts the moral right to be identified as the author of this work.

Ashley Atwood has no responsibility for the persistence or accuracy of URLs for external or third-party Internet Websites referred to in this publication and does not guarantee that any content on such Websites is, or will remain, accurate or appropriate.

Designations used by companies to distinguish their products are often claimed as trademarks. All brand names and product names used in this book and on its cover are trade names, service marks, trademarks and registered trademarks of their respective owners. The publishers and the book are not associated with any product or vendor mentioned in this book. None of the companies referenced within the book have endorsed the book.

First edition

This book was professionally typeset on Reedsy.
Find out more at reedsy.com

This book is dedicated to my firstborn. He has sacrificed time with his mom his whole life as I fight to pursue careers that demands work 24/7. As I watch him mold into a young man, my prayers for him are best said by the talented Rascal Flats: "That this life becomes all that you want it to. Your dreams stay big, your worries stay small...and while you're out there getting where you're getting to, I hope you know somebody loves you and wants the same things too."

I love you.

Wanderlust:
(n.) a strong desire for or impulse to wander or travel and explore the world

Preface

Welcome to Phoenix! My name is Ashley Atwood, and I'm a local Realtor with My Home Group. My company, Sunshine Hill Properties, owns and manages many short and mid-term rentals across the valley, and my guests constantly ask about fun things to do or the best places to eat.

I wrote this book with my highly valued guests in mind. I want them to have the most incredible experiences during their stay. Then, I realized I wanted to hear about their specific experiences at each destination. That's when I decided to make this book into a journal!

During your stay, as you remember your sun-soaked day at Lake Pleasant or the comedy show you saw that almost made you pee your pants, write it down to keep as part of your memory book.

This book is meant for my guests to be able to customize their stay here in Phoenix. So, if you're looking for a nice date night, flip to the restaurant section, or if the kids are driving you up the wall in the summer heat, flip to see some of the fantastic indoor family-friendly attractions Phoenix offers. I tried to find something for everyone all over the Valley.

I can't wait to have this book on every coffee table of my rentals, and a signed copy will definitely be in the housewarming basket for my real estate clients. I hope you can create fond memories with your friends and family during your stay in Phoenix and use this book to cherish them forever!

If you're visiting one of the spots I recommended, tag me on Instagram

@SusnhineHill_Properties, and maybe I'll see you around town!

Table of Contents

Chapter 1: Introduction to Phoenix

Chapter 2: Arts and Culture
Museums

- Arizona Heritage Center at Papago Park
- Heard Museum Phoenix Art Museum
- S'edav Va'aki Museum
- Arizona Science Center
- Children's Museum of Phoenix
- Musical Instrument Museum
- Wonderspaces Arizona
- Arizona Commemorative Air Force Museum
- Hall of Flame Museum of Firefighting
- Penske Racing Museum

Performing Arts and Theatres

- Arizona Opera
- Arizona Theatre Company
- ASU Gammage
- Ballet Arizona
- Great Arizona Puppet Theater
- Orpheum Theatre
- The Phoenix Symphony
- The Phoenix Theatre Company

- Theatre Artists Studio
- Valley Youth Theatre

Old Town Scottsdale

- Restaurants
- Bars & Clubs
- Shopping

Roosevelt Row

- Top Spots
- Art Walk

Chapter 3: Hiking, Camping & Outdoor Activities

- Outdoor Safety Tips

Hiking

Easy

- Double Butte Loop and Hole-in-the-Rock Trail in Papago Park
- Blevins Trail in Usery Mountain Regional Park
- Waterfall Trail in White Tank Mountain Regional Park
- Phoenix South Mountian Loop in South Mountain Preserve

Moderate

- Hidden Valley via Mormon Trail in South Mountain Park/Preserve
- Pinnacle Peak Trail in Pinnacle Peak Park
- Lookout Mountain Summit Trail in Phoenix Mountain Preserve
- Dixie Mountain Loop in the Phoenix Sonoran Desert Preserve

Difficult

- Echo Canyon Trail on Camelback Mountain
- Tom's Thumb Trail South in the McDowell Sonoran Preserve
- Piestewa Peak Summit Trail #300 in Phoenix Mountain Preserve
- Flatiron via Siphon Draw Trail in Lost Dutchman State Park

Lakes

- Lake Pleasant Regional Park
- Saguaro Lake
- Canyon Lake
- Apache Lake
- Roosevelt Lake

Camping

- Estrella Mountain Regional Park
- Lost Dutchman State Park
- Lake Pleasant Regional Park
- White Tank Mountain Regional Park
- McDowell Mountain Regional Park

Chapter 4: Activities
Nightlife

- Monarch Theatre
- Crescent Ballroom - Themes
- Club Dwntwn - Latin
- Charlie's - LGBTQ
- Tru Ultra Lounge - Hip Hop
- Rip's Bar - Casual
- Scottin' Boots Dance Hall - Country/Western

Aquariums/Zoos

- Out of Africa Wildlife Park
- Bearzona Wildlife Park
- OdySea Aquarium
- Phoenix Zoo
- Sea Life Arizona
- Wildlife World Zoo & Aquarium

Kids

- I.d.e.a. Museum
- Golfland Sunsplash
- Butterfly Wonderland
- Crayola Experience
- Gold Field Ghost Town & Mine Tours
- McCormick-Stillman Railroad Park

Theme Parks & Water Parks

- Lego Land Discovery Center
- Six Flags Hurricane Harbor
- Great Wolf Lodge
- Enchanted Island Amusement Park

Botanical Garden

- Desert Botanical Garden
- Japanese Friendship Garden
- Boyce Thompson Arboretum
- USS Arizona Memorial Gardens at Salt River

Adventuring

- Rock Climbing:
- Hot Air Ballooning
- ATV Rentals

Shopping

- Local
- Frances
- Time Bomb Vintage
- Changing Hands Bookstore
- Arizona Hiking Shack
- Michael Todd's Treasures
- For The People
- Now or Never

Farmers Markets

- Downtown Phoenix Farmers Market
- Uptown Farmers Market
- Tempe Farmers Market
- Singh Meadows Farmers Market
- Park West Farmer's Market

Shopping Centers

- Biltmore Fashion Square
- Scottsdale Quarter
- The Shops at Gainey Village
- Westgate Glendale
- Melrose District
- Arizona Mills Mall

Spas

- Joya Spa
- Alvorado Spa at Royal Palms
- Phoenician Spa
- Hawaiian Experience Spa
- The Spa at the Victory Club

Fitness

- Yoga - Urban Yoga Phoenix
- Pilates - Remedy Pilates and Barre
- HIIT - Frame
- Martial Arts - MMA Lab
- Boxing - Rumble Boxing
- Cycling - Sweatshop on Central

Chapter 5: Sports and Gaming

- NBA
- NFL
- MLB
- Spring Training
- NHL
- Waste Management Phoenix Open
- Golf
- Casinos
- ASU
- Journal Prompts

Chapter 6: Restaurants, Bars, & Bakeries
Casual Fare

- Danky's BBQ
- The Stand

- Matt's Big Breakfast
- The Vig
- Cuff

Cultural Menus

- Italian
- Mexican
- Sushi
- Thai
- Chinese
- Indian
- Greek

Farm to Table

- Quiessence at the Farm
- True Food Kitchen
- Blue Hound Kitchen & Cocktails
- The Farm at South Mountain
- Flower Child

Fine Dining

- Steak 44
- Binkleys
- Tarbell's
- Different Point of View
- Ocean Prime

Craft Beer & Local Wine

- OHSO Brewery

- Turquoise Wine Cellar and Tasting Room
- Huss Brewing Co & Taproom
- Pedal Haus Brewery
- Arizona Stronghold

Food Trucks

- AZ Feastivals
- Ahwatukee Eats
- Food Truck Friday West
- First Friday West Valley

Kid Friendly

- The Morning Squeeze
- Someburros
- Chelsea's Kitchen
- Ruslter's Rooste
- Luci's at the Orchard

Patios and Rooftops

- Culinary Dropout
- The Churchill
- Eden Rooftop Bar
- Upstairs at Flint
- Hash Kitchen/Sicilian Butcher

Desserts and Bakeries

- Boyer Bakery
- The Yard Milkshake Bar
- Beignet Babe

- Voodoo Donuts
- Urban Cookies Bakeshop

Coffee

- Ebb & Flow
- Bad Ass Coffee of Hawaii
- Driftwood Coffee Co
- The Human Bean
- Renegade Coffee Co

Chapter 7: Day Trips from Phoenix

- Sedona
- Jerome
- Bisbee
- Flagstaff
- Grand Canyon
- Tombstone
- Rocky Point, Mexico

Chapter 8: Practical Information and Resources
Transportation options in Phoenix

- Valleymetro.org
- Valley Metro Rail
- Phoenix Transit Bus
- Phoenix Dial-a-Ride
- Turo and Car Rentals
- Uber, Taxi, and Limo Services

Accommodation recommendations for every budget

- My Rentals
- Hotels
- RV Parks

Safety Tips
  Reference Map

1

Introduction to Phoenix

A Brief History

The history of Phoenix, AZ, is a tale of resilience, adaptation, and growth. The area's recorded history dates back to ancient Native American civilizations, including the Hohokam people, who settled along the Salt River around 300 AD. They built an extensive irrigation canal system, allowing them to cultivate crops in the dry desert.

In the mid-1800s, the region was part of Mexico. And in 1848, the Treaty of Guadalupe Hidalgo ceded the land to the United States after the US-Mexico War. The Gadsden Purchase in 1853 further expanded the territory, including present-day Phoenix.

The city's modern history began in 1867 when Jack Swilling, a Confederate veteran, recognized the potential of the ancient Hohokam canal system and founded a small farming community in the area. He named it "Phoenix" after the mythical bird rising from its ashes, symbolizing the rebirth of a civilization.

Soon after, in 1881, the railroad reached Phoenix, leading to a significant population increase and further economic growth. Then finally 1911, Phoenix officially became the capital of the newly admitted state of Arizona.

The city's economy boomed during World War II when military installations, such as Luke Air Force Base and Williams Field, were established.

After the war, Phoenix evolved into a major industrial and agricultural hub, attracting migrants seeking employment and opportunities.

Today, Phoenix is the fifth-largest city in the United States and a thriving metropolis, boasting a diverse population, a rich cultural scene, and a strong economy anchored in technology, healthcare, and tourism.

The history of Phoenix serves as a reminder of human adaptability in harsh environments, transforming a once arid landscape into a vibrant urban center that continues to attract people from all walks of life.

A Vibrant Desert City

Today, Phoenix is known as the "Valley of the Sun" and is a vibrant city dancing with the spirit of the Southwest. Blending the burning desert sunsets with cultural diversity and flourishing urban life, Phoenix offers unique and mesmerizing experiences to all that experience it. At the Sonoran Desert's heart, Phoenix is drenched in sunshine and surrounded by Mountain Views. Our backdrop attracts outdoor enthusiasts from far and wide to explore all Phoenix offers. Most prominently, we boast over 41,000 acres of protected land, including the McDowell Sonoran Preserve, South Mountain Park, and Papago Park, to name a few.

Embracing our Southwestern Culture and nurturing diversity and creativity, the art scene has blossomed from street art to galleries, museums, and theaters. You'll quickly find something to suit your tastes and experience some of the newest creators hitting the scene. The artists also include a thriving culinary experience to fulfill any indulgence. From fine dining to food trucks, or boutique dessert shops, your tastebuds will be mesmerized from start to finish.

What major metropolitan area would be complete without a selection of sports arenas? Major League Baseball, the National Football League, and the National Basketball Association have incredible stadiums to catch a game of your choice. But my favorites are the spring training baseball games mimicking a small-town feel with big-time players.

Climate

Phoenix is best known for its long, scorching summers and beautifully mild winters. With over 300 days of sunshine annually, we are an ideal destination for those seeking refuge from the cold and snow. Summers are sweltering and regularly exceed 100 degrees F (38 degrees C). Staying hydrated, seeking shade, and planning indoor activities from June through September is essential. The best part of summer is the monsoon season; these sporadic thunderstorms bring relief from the heat and light up the desert sky with vibrant red, purple, and orange colors during sunset or dancing lightning shows in the clouds at night. For outdoor adventure seekers, October through May brings more moderate temperatures and far better mountain biking, hiking, and golfing conditions. With our winters ranging in temperatures between 60 degrees F (15-20 degrees C) to 40 degrees F (4-9 degrees C), Phoenix is a top destination for a population called "Snowbirds" who fly south and escape shoveling snow from their driveways.

2

Arts and Culture

MUSEUMS

AZ Heritage Center at Papago Park

The AZ Heritage Center at Papago Park is a captivating museum in Tempe, Arizona, that delves into the rich history and culture of the state. Located within the picturesque Papago Park, the center offers visitors an immersive experience through interactive exhibits, artifacts, and engaging displays. From the stories of Native American tribes to the growth of Arizona as a state, the museum showcases the diverse heritage and contributions of the region. The Center also hosts educational programs, events, and workshops that provide a deeper understanding of Arizona's past and its impact on the present.

1300 N College Ave Tempe, AZ 85288

(480) 929-0292

Tickets: Children Under 6 are free; others range from $7-$15

Museum Hours: Tuesday-Saturday, 10 am-2 pm

Library & Archives: Tuesday-Friday 10 am-2 pm by appointment only ahsreference@azhs.gov to schedule.

https://arizonahistoricalsociety.org/museum/arizona-heritage-center/

ARTS AND CULTURE

Heard Museum

The Heard Museum in Phoenix, Arizona, is a renowned institution dedicated to showcasing the art, culture, and history of Native American peoples. Founded in 1929, the museum features an extensive collection of Native American art, including pottery, textiles, jewelry, and contemporary artworks. With a focus on promoting understanding and appreciation of Indigenous cultures, the Heard Museum offers engaging exhibits, educational programs, and events that highlight the diverse traditions and contributions of Native American communities. It serves as a vital resource for both locals and visitors, fostering cultural exchange and preserving the heritage of Native American peoples.

2301 N. Central Ave. Phoenix, AZ 85004
(602) 252-8840
Tickets: Children under 6 and American Indian Citizens are Free; Others range from $9-$22.50
Hours: Tuesday-Sunday, 10 am-4 pm
www.heard.org

Phoenix Art Museum

Established in 1959, The Phoenix Art Museum is a prominent cultural institution in Phoenix. With its extensive collection and diverse exhibits, the museum offers a captivating experience for art enthusiasts. Visitors can explore artworks spanning various periods, styles, and mediums, including paintings, sculptures, photography, and more. The museum showcases renowned artists such as Frida Kahlo, Georgia O'Keeffe, and Pablo Picasso while highlighting local and regional talents. The Phoenix Art Museum also hosts educational programs, lectures, and special events that provide deeper insights into the art world. It is a hub for creativity, inspiration, and cultural enrichment, making it a must-visit destination for art lovers in Phoenix.

1625 N. Central Ave., Central Ave., and McDowell Rd. Phoenix, AZ 85004
(602) 257-1880

Tickets: Children under 5 free; Others range from $5-$25; Memberships Available

Hours: Wednesdays 10am-9pm (Pay what you wish from 3pm-9pm) Thursday-Sunday 10am-5pm

www.phxart.org

S'edav Va'aki Museum

Formerly Known as the Pueblo Grande Museum, the S'edav Va'aki Museum is the largest preserved archaeological site in Phoenix. Enjoy a 2/3 mile (1 km) hike through this ancient site once inhabited by the Hohokam culture dating back to 500 AD. Since this is a protected site, etiquette rules must be followed. Visit the website for details.

4619 E. Washington St. Phoenix, AZ 85034

(602) 495-0901

Tickets: Children under 6 are free; Others range from $3-$6.

Hours: October-April Monday-Saturday 9 am-4:45 pm, Sunday 1 pm-4:45 pm

May-September Tuesday-Saturday 9 am-4:45 pm

https://www.phoenix.gov/parks/arts-culture-history/sedav-vaaki

Arizona Science Center

The Arizona Science Center in Phoenix is a captivating destination that combines education, entertainment, and exploration. With hands-on exhibits, interactive displays, and engaging demonstrations, the center offers a dynamic and immersive experience for visitors of all ages. The center covers a wide range of scientific disciplines, from the wonders of space to the marvels of the human body. Visitors can also enjoy planetarium shows, IMAX movies and participate in educational programs and workshops. The Arizona Science Center is where curiosity is sparked, and learning becomes an exciting adventure, making it a must-visit attraction for science enthusiasts and curious minds.

600 E. Washington St. Phoenix, AZ 85004
(602) 716-2000
Tickets: Children under 3 are free; Others range from $15.95-$21.95
Parking Not Included
Hours: Monday-Sunday, 10 am-4 pm
www.azscience.org

Children's Museum of Phoenix

The Children's Museum of Phoenix is a vibrant and interactive museum designed specifically for children. Located in downtown Phoenix, it offers many exhibits and activities that promote learning, creativity and play. Children can explore themed areas, including a construction zone, a market, a sensory room, and a multi-level climber. The museum encourages hands-on exploration and imaginative play, allowing children to engage in educational experiences while having fun. With its focus on interactive exhibits and child-centered programming, the Children's Museum of Phoenix provides a stimulating and engaging environment for young visitors to learn, discover, and grow.

215 N. 7th St. Phoenix, AZ 85034
(602) 253-0501
Tickets: Children under 1 are free; Others are $17. Memberships Available.
Hours: Summer Hours (Memorial Day-Labor Day) Monday-Sunday, 9 am-4 pm
www.childrensmuseumofphoenix.org

Musical Instrument Museum

The Musical Instrument Museum (MIM) in Phoenix is a one-of-a-kind institution that celebrates the diversity and beauty of music worldwide. With a collection of over 7,000 musical instruments from cultures around the globe, the museum offers a unique and immersive experience for music enthusiasts. Visitors can explore exhibits showcasing instruments from different cultures, listen to their sounds, and learn about each instrument's history and cultural significance. The MIM also hosts live performances, educational programs, and interactive displays, providing a captivating and educational journey through the world of music. Check the website for concerts during your trip.

4725 E. Mayo Blvd.Phoenix, AZ 85050

(480) 478-6000

Tickets: Children under 3 are free; Others range from $10-$20

Hours: Monday-Saturday, 9 am-5 pm; Sunday, 10 am-5 pm

www.mim.org

Wonderspaces Arizona

Wonderspaces Arizona is an innovative and immersive art experience located in Scottsdale. As a traveling art show, it features a curated selection of interactive and awe-inspiring artworks from around the world. Visitors are encouraged to engage with the installations, stepping into vibrant, transformative environments that challenge perception and spark wonder. Wonderspaces Arizona provides a platform for both established and emerging artists to showcase their creations and offers a unique opportunity for audiences to explore the boundaries of art. With its ever-changing exhibitions, Wonderspaces Arizona continuously delivers fresh and captivating experiences that ignite the imagination and leave a lasting impact.

7014 E. Camelback Rd., Ste. 584, Scottsdale Fashion Sq.Scottsdale, AZ 85251

Tickets: Children under 3 are free; Others range from $15-$24; Memberships Available

Hours: Monday-Friday, 12 pm-10 pm; Saturday, 10 am-10 pm; Sunday, 11 am-7 pm

www.arizona.wonderspaces.com

ARTS AND CULTURE

Arizona Commemorative Air Force Museum

The Arizona Commemorative Air Force (CAF) Museum in Mesa, Arizona, is a captivating destination for aviation enthusiasts and history buffs. The museum showcases a remarkable collection of vintage aircraft, including World War II-era planes, helicopters, and other military aircraft. Visitors can explore these beautifully restored aircraft up close and learn about their historical significance. The Arizona CAF Museum also offers immersive experiences, such as aircraft tours and flight experiences, allowing visitors to step back in time and get a glimpse into the heroic stories of the men and women who served in the Air Force. It's a must-visit destination for anyone passionate about aviation and military history.

   2017 N. Greenfield Rd.Mesa, AZ 85215
   (480) 924-1940
   Tickets: Children under 5 are free; Others range from $5-$15
   Hours: Thursday-Saturday, 10 am-4 pm
   www.azcaf.org

Hall of Flame Museum of Firefighting

The Hall of Flame (get it) Museum of Firefighting is a captivating tribute to the bravery and history of firefighting. With its extensive collection of firefighting artifacts, including vintage fire engines, equipment, uniforms, and memorabilia, the museum offers visitors a unique insight into the world of firefighting. The exhibits showcase the evolution of firefighting techniques and technology and the heroic stories of firefighters throughout history. The Hall of Flame Museum provides an educational and immersive experience for visitors of all ages, honoring the courage and sacrifice of those who protect our communities from fire.

   6101 E. Van Buren St.Phoenix, AZ 85008
   (602) 275-3473
   Tickets: Children under 3 are free; Others range from $10-$17
   Hours: Tuesday-Saturday, 10 am-6 pm

www.hallofflame.org

Penske Racing Museum

The Penske Racing Museum in Phoenix, Arizona, is a thrilling destination for motorsports enthusiasts. Located on the Penske Corporation headquarters grounds, the museum showcases a remarkable collection of racing cars, trophies, and memorabilia from Team Penske's storied history in motorsports. Visitors can explore an impressive array of Indy cars, NASCAR vehicles, sports cars, and other racing machines that have played a pivotal role in Team Penske's success. The museum provides a unique opportunity to learn about the team's accomplishments, experience the thrill of racing, and gain insight into the world of motorsports. It's a must-visit destination for fans of speed and competition.

7191 E. Chauncey Ln.Phoenix, AZ 85054
(480) 538-4444
Tickets: Free!
Hours: Monday-Saturday, 10 am 4 pm; Sunday, 12 pm-5 pm
www.penskeautomall.com

PERFORMING ARTS

Arizona Opera

The Arizona Opera is a prestigious performing arts organization that brings opera's beauty and drama to Arizona audiences. Founded in 1971, the company stages various operatic productions, showcasing classic and contemporary works. With a talented roster of singers, directors, and musicians, the Arizona Opera delivers captivating performances that combine stunning vocals, powerful storytelling, and elaborate set designs. The company's commitment to artistic excellence and community engagement has made it a vital cultural institution in Arizona's arts landscape. Whether you're an opera aficionado or new to the genre, the

Arizona Opera offers unforgettable experiences that transport audiences into the world of grand opera.

  1636 N. Central Ave.Phoenix, AZ 85004

  (602) 218-7321

  www.azopera.org

Arizona Theatre Company

The Arizona Theatre Company (ATC) is a dynamic and esteemed theater company that enriches Arizona's cultural landscape. Founded in 1967, ATC produces diverse theatrical productions, including classic plays, contemporary works, musicals, and world premieres. With a talented ensemble of actors, directors, and designers, ATC delivers captivating performances that showcase the power of storytelling and the magic of live theater. The company is dedicated to artistic excellence, community engagement, and nurturing local talent through educational programs. From thought-provoking dramas to joyous musicals, the Arizona Theatre Company offers audiences transformative theatrical experiences that resonate long after the final curtain falls.

  222 E. Monroe St.Phoenix, AZ 85004

  (602) 256-6899

  www.atc.org

Arizona State University Gammage

ASU Gammage, located on the campus of Arizona State University in Tempe, is a renowned performing arts center that has become a cultural landmark in Arizona. The venue is designed by famed architect Frank Lloyd Wright and boasts distinctive and visually striking architecture. ASU Gammage hosts diverse performances, including Broadway shows, musicals, dance performances, concerts, and more. With its state-of-the-art facilities and top-notch productions, ASU Gammage attracts acclaimed artists and provides a platform for world-class performances. The venue's commitment to arts education and community engagement makes it a hub for creativity, inspiration, and artistic excellence in the Phoenix metropolitan area.

   1200 S. Forest Ave., Arizona State University Tempe, AZ 85287

   (480) 965-3434

   www.asugammage.com

Ballet Arizona

Ballet Arizona is a premier ballet company that captivates audiences with artistry, grace, and precision. Based in Phoenix, the company showcases a diverse repertoire, from classical ballets to contemporary works, performed by a talented ensemble of dancers. With its commitment to artistic excellence, Ballet Arizona presents captivating performances that blend technical prowess with emotional storytelling. The company also engages with the community through educational outreach programs, bringing the beauty and joy of ballet to people of all ages. Ballet Arizona's dedication to the art form and its ability to transport audiences into a world of beauty and expression make it a shining star in the dance world.

   2835 E. Washington St.Phoenix, AZ 85034

   (602) 381-1096

   www.balletaz.org

Great Arizona Puppet Theater

The Great Arizona Puppet Theater is a beloved cultural institution that brings joy and imagination to audiences of all ages. Located in Phoenix, the theater presents enchanting puppet shows that weave together storytelling, music, and artistry. The talented puppeteers bring characters to life, engaging audiences in magical tales and captivating performances. From classic stories to original productions, the Great Arizona Puppet Theater delights and educates children and adults alike. The theater also offers educational programs, workshops, and special events, further fostering a love for the puppetry arts. It's a place where imagination knows no bounds, and the wonder of puppetry takes center stage.

302 W. Latham St.Phoenix, AZ 85003

(602) 262-2050

www.azpuppets.org

Orpheum Theatre

The Orpheum Theatre, located in downtown Phoenix, is a historic and iconic venue that showcases a wide array of performing arts. Built in 1929, the theater's elegant architecture and opulent interiors transport visitors to a bygone era. It has served as a platform for various performances, including Broadway shows, concerts, ballets, and more. The Orpheum Theatre's rich history and grandeur create a captivating atmosphere that enhances the experience of each performance. With its commitment to preserving its architectural heritage and presenting high-quality productions, the Orpheum Theatre continues to be a cultural gem that delights audiences and fosters a love for the performing arts.

203 W. Adams St.Phoenix, AZ 85003

(602) 262-6225

www.orpheumphx.com

The Phoenix Symphony

The Phoenix Symphony is a renowned orchestra that has captivated audiences for over 70 years. With its exceptional musicians and world-class performances, the Symphony delivers breathtaking renditions of classical masterpieces, contemporary compositions, and pop concerts. From symphonies and concertos to film scores and collaborations with renowned guest artists, The Phoenix Symphony offers diverse musical experiences that inspire and engage listeners. The Symphony also provides educational programs, outreach initiatives, and community concerts, fostering a love for orchestral music and enriching the cultural fabric of Phoenix. The Phoenix Symphony continues to be a shining beacon of musical excellence in Arizona's vibrant arts landscape.

   1 N. 1st St., Ste. 200Phoenix, AZ 85004

   (602) 495-1999

   www.phoenixsymphony.org

The Phoenix Theatre Company

The Phoenix Theatre Company is a dynamic and acclaimed theater company that has been a pillar of the arts community in Phoenix for over 100 years. The company is committed to excellence and stages a diverse range of productions, including classic plays, contemporary works, musicals, and world premieres. The Phoenix Theatre Company showcases top-tier talent onstage and behind the scenes, providing audiences with compelling performances, innovative storytelling, and incredible production values. In addition to its mainstage productions, the company also offers educational programs, workshops, and community outreach initiatives, nurturing the next generation of theater artists and fostering a deep appreciation for the performing arts.

   1825 N. Central Ave.Phoenix, AZ 85004

   (602) 254-2151

   www.phoenixtheatre.com

Theatre Artists Studio

Theatre Artists Studio is a respected and intimate theater company in Scottsdale. Founded in 1993, the studio provides a platform for professional and emerging playwrights, actors, and directors to showcase their talents and bring compelling stories to life. With its focus on producing thought-provoking and innovative works, Theatre Artists Studio presents a diverse range of productions that challenge and engage audiences. The company also offers educational programs and workshops, nurturing the development of theater artists and cultivating a vibrant arts community. Theatre Artists Studio is a haven for creativity and collaboration, making it a destination for theater enthusiasts seeking unique and enriching experiences.

   12406 N. Paradise Village Pkwy EastScottsdale, AZ 85254

   (602) 765-0120

   www.thestudiophx.org

Valley Youth Theatre

Valley Youth Theatre (VYT) is a vibrant and renowned theater company dedicated to empowering young performers in Phoenix, Arizona. Established in 1989, VYT provides a platform for young actors, ages 7 to 19, to showcase their talents in professional-quality productions. The company offers a wide range of training programs, classes, and performance opportunities that nurture aspiring theater artists' artistic growth and development. With its commitment to inclusivity and fostering a love for the performing arts, Valley Youth Theatre creates an environment where young performers can thrive, build confidence, and cultivate a lifelong appreciation for theater.

   525 N. 1st St.Phoenix, AZ 85004

   (602) 253-8188

   www.vyt.com

OLD TOWN SCOTTSDALE

Old Town Scottsdale, located in the heart of the city, is a vibrant and historic district that embodies the charm and character of Arizona's past. With its mix of Western heritage, art galleries, boutiques, restaurants, and cultural attractions, Old Town Scottsdale offers a unique and immersive experience.

   One of the main draws of Old Town Scottsdale is its Old West ambiance. The area is known for its wooden sidewalks, rustic buildings, and Western-themed storefronts that harken back to the days of cowboys and saloons. Visitors can explore the Scottsdale Museum of the West, which showcases the art and history of the American West, or take a stroll along Main Street to browse Western art galleries and shops.

Art enthusiasts will be delighted by the numerous art galleries scattered throughout Old Town. From contemporary works to Native American art, the district is a hub for creativity and expression. The weekly Thursday night ArtWalk, where galleries open their doors to the public, is a popular event showcasing the area's vibrant art scene.

Food lovers will also find a diverse culinary scene in Old Town Scottsdale. From upscale dining establishments to trendy cafes and local food joints, the district offers a range of dining options to suit every palate. Visitors can savor Southwestern cuisine, international flavors, and craft cocktails in the district's many eateries.

Old Town Scottsdale hosts various events and festivals, such as the Scottsdale Art Festival and the Parada del Sol, a Western-themed parade and rodeo. These events unite the community and celebrate the region's culture and unique heritage.

In conclusion, Old Town Scottsdale is a captivating district that blends history, art, and a lively atmosphere. With its Western charm, art galleries, diverse dining scene, and vibrant events, Old Town Scottsdale offers a delightful and enriching experience for locals and visitors.

The following recommendations are in no particular order and are the top spots for Old Town Scottsdale. Please check the websites for the most current information!

Restaurants

FnB
American $$$
7125 E 5th Ave #31, Scottsdale, AZ 85251
(480) 284-4777
www.fnbrestaurant.com

Cafe Monarch
Fine Dining $$$$
6939 E 1st Ave, Scottsdale, AZ 85251

(480) 970-7682
www.cafemonarch.com

Citizen Public House
American $$$
7111 E 5th Ave, Scottsdale, AZ 85251
(480) 398-4208
www.citizenpublichouse.com

Virtu Honest Craft
American $$$
3701 N Marshall Way, Scottsdale, AZ 85251
(480) 946-3477
www.virtuhonestcraft.com/hub

The Mission Old Town
Latin American $$$
3815 N Brown Ave, Scottsdale, AZ 85251
(480) 636-5005
www.themissionaz.com

Olive & Ivy Restaurant & Marketplace
American $$
7135 E Camelback Rd Ste 195, Scottsdale, AZ 85251
(480) 751-2200
hwww.oliveandivyrestaurant.com

Culinary Dropout
American $$
7135 E Camelback Rd Ste 123, Scottsdale, AZ 85251
(480) 970-1700
www.culinarydropout.com

The House Brasserie
Fine Dining $$$
6936 E Main St, Scottsdale, AZ 85251
(480) 634-1600
www.thehousebrasserie.com

Sel
American $$$$
7044 E Main St, Scottsdale, AZ 85251
(480) 949-6296
www.selrestaurant.com

The Canal Club
Cuban $$$
4925 N Scottsdale Rd, Scottsdale, AZ 85251
(480) 424-6095
www.thecanalclubaz.com

Bars and Clubs

Bottled Blonde
Pizzeria & Bar $$
7340 E Indian Plaza #100, Scottsdale, AZ 85251
(480) 970-1112
bottledblondepizzeria.com

The Beverly on Main
Cocktail Bar $$
7018 E Main St, Scottsdale, AZ 85251
(480) 889-5580
www.beverlyonmain.com

ARTS AND CULTURE

Riot House
 Night Club
 3411, 4425 N Saddlebag Trail #105, Scottsdale, AZ 852514
 (480) 935-5910
 www.riothouse.com

The Rusty Spur Saloon
 Bar $
 7245 E Main St, Scottsdale, AZ 85251
 (480) 425-7787
 rustyspursaloon.com

Dierks Bentley's Whiskey Row
 Bar and Grill $$
 4420 N Saddlebag Trail, Scottsdale, AZ 85251
 (480) 945-4200
 www.dierkswhiskeyrow.com

Maya Dayclub
 Dance Club $$
 7333 E Indian Plaza, Scottsdale, AZ 85251
 (480) 625-0528
 mayaclubaz.com

El Hefe
 Taqueria $$
 4425 N Saddlebag Trail #101, Scottsdale, AZ 85251
 (480) 945-6200
 www.elhefe.com

Wasted Grain
 Live Music & Bar $$
 7295 E Stetson Dr, Scottsdale, AZ 85251

(480) 970-0500
www.wastedgrain.com

Social Tap Eatery
Bar & Grill $$
4312 N Brown Ave, Scottsdale, AZ 85251
(602) 432-6719
www.socialtapscottsdaleaz.com

Hi-Fi Kitchen & Cocktails
Bar $$
4420 N Saddlebag Trail, Scottsdale, AZ 85251
(480) 970-5000
www.hifibars.com

Shopping

Scottsdale Fashion Square
7014 E Camelback Rd, Scottsdale, AZ 85251
(480) 941-2140
www.fashionsquare.com

Fifth Avenue Shops
E 5th Ave, Scottsdale, AZ 85251
www.oldtownscottsdale.com/business-categories/5th-avenue-shops/

Scottsdale Waterfront
7135 E Camelback Rd, Scottsdale, AZ 85251
(833) 800-4343
www.scottsdalewaterfront.shopkimco.com

Marshall Way Arts District
4243 N Marshall Way, Scottsdale, AZ 85251

ARTS AND CULTURE

Scottsdale Mercantile
3965 N Brown Ave, Scottsdale, AZ 85251
(480) 590-2699
www.merchantile.co

ROOSEVELT ROW

Roosevelt Row, also known as RoRo, is a vibrant and eclectic arts district in downtown Phoenix. Stretching along Roosevelt Street between 7th Street and Central Avenue, this creative hub is a thriving community of artists, galleries, studios, shops, and restaurants.

Roosevelt Row is renowned for its dynamic street art scene. Colorful murals adorn the sides of buildings, alleys, and even electrical boxes, transforming the area into an open-air art gallery. The district also hosts the annual "Roosevelt Row Chile Pepper Festival," where local artists showcase their talents and celebrate the neighborhood's vibrant culture.

In addition to street art, Roosevelt Row is home to numerous galleries and artist studios. Visitors can explore contemporary art exhibitions, attend art walks, and even engage with artists directly during open studio events. This lively atmosphere encourages artistic expression, dialogue, and community engagement.

Beyond the art, Roosevelt Row offers an array of independent shops, boutiques, and vintage stores. Visitors can discover unique clothing, accessories, home decor, and more while supporting local businesses.

The district's culinary scene is equally enticing, with various restaurants, cafes, and food trucks serving diverse and delectable cuisine. From farm-to-table eateries to international flavors, Roosevelt Row satisfies every palate.

Roosevelt Row is a destination for art and shopping and a gathering place for community events, live music performances, and cultural festivals. It embodies the spirit of creativity, innovation, and collaboration, making it a must-visit destination for those seeking a deep, immersive art experience in Phoenix. The following recommendations are in no particular order and are the top spots for Old Town Scottsdale. Please check the websites for the most current information and see an updated and complete list at www.rooseveltrow.org

Jobot Coffee & Bar

A popular coffee shop and diner offering a cozy atmosphere and delicious fare.

333 E Roosevelt St, Phoenix, AZ 85004

(602) 820-9505

www.facebook.com/jobotcoffeeandbar

Welcome Diner

A local favorite serving up comfort food with a modern twist, known for their fantastic burgers and pies.

929 E Pierce St, Phoenix, AZ 85006

(602) 495-1111

www.welcomediner.net

Changing Hands Bookstore

An independent bookstore that hosts author events and offers a wide selection of books, gifts, and more.

300 W Camelback Rd, Phoenix, AZ 85013

(602) 274-0067

www.changinghands.com

Valley Bar

An underground bar and live music venue that hosts a diverse range of performances.

130 N Central Ave, Phoenix, AZ 85004

(602) 716-2222

www.valleybarphx.com

The Lost Leaf

A unique bar with an extensive selection of craft beers and a cozy patio space.

914 N 5th St, Phoenix, AZ 85004

(602) 258-0014

www.thelostleaf.org

Carly's Bistro

A neighborhood bistro and Bar known for its relaxed atmosphere and live music events.

128 E Roosevelt St, Phoenix, AZ 85004

(602) 262-2759

www.carlysbistro.com

Phoenix General

A boutique offering curated clothing, accessories, and home goods from local and independent designers.

214 E Roosevelt St, Phoenix, AZ 85004

(623) 248-8686

www.phxgeneral.com

First Fridays Art Walk

Phoenix's First Fridays Art Walk is a celebrated monthly event transforming the downtown area into a bustling hub of creativity and artistic expression. On the first Friday of every month, art enthusiasts, locals, and visitors gather to explore an array of galleries, studios, and pop-up art spaces.

The Art Walk stretches along Roosevelt Row and the surrounding streets, creating a vibrant and energetic atmosphere. Galleries and venues open their doors, showcasing a rich tapestry of artistic mediums, including paintings, sculptures, photography, mixed media, and more. The Art Walk provides a platform for established and emerging artists to exhibit their work, fostering community and dialogue among creators and art enthusiasts.

Beyond the visual arts, the Art Walk also features live music performances, street performers, food trucks, and vendors selling various crafts and artisanal products. The eclectic mix of sights, sounds, and flavors creates a captivating sensory experience.

First Fridays Art Walk is not only about appreciating art but also about connecting with the local community. It offers an opportunity to engage with artists, gain insight into their creative process, and even purchase directly from the creators. Visitors can immerse themselves in the lively street scene, meet fellow art enthusiasts, and celebrate Phoenix's vibrant arts culture.

With its vibrant atmosphere, a diverse range of art, and community spirit, the First Fridays Art Walk has become a beloved institution in Phoenix, bringing together artists and art lovers to celebrate the power of creativity and expression.

3

Hiking, Camping & Outdoor Activities

This chapter is filled with outdoor activities, and most parks overlap with an abundance of family-friendly fun. You'll easily combine hiking, camping, and water sports in one weekend trip if that's your goal. Please use this chapter to customize your unique experience.

Outdoor Safety Tips

When venturing into the outdoors in Phoenix, Arizona, it's essential to be prepared and mindful of safety precautions to maximize the enjoyment of your adventure. Here are some outdoor safety tips for exploring the Phoenix area:

1. Stay hydrated: The desert climate in Phoenix can be scorching hot and dry. Carry an ample supply of water and drink frequently to prevent dehydration. It's recommended to drink at least one gallon of water per day when engaging in outdoor activities.
2. Dress appropriately: Wear lightweight, breathable clothing and a wide-brimmed hat to protect yourself from sunscreen generously and reapply as needed. Wear long sleeves and pants to shield yourself from the sun's rays.
3. Be mindful of wildlife: Arizona is home to diverse wildlife, including

snakes, and scorpions. Be cautious when hiking or exploring natural areas, watch your step, and avoid reaching into crevices or under rocks.
4. Plan ahead: Research the trail or area you plan to visit before embarking on outdoor activities. Check weather conditions, trail difficulty, and any potential hazards. Inform someone of your plans, including your expected time of return.
5. Stay on designated trails: Stick to established trails and avoid venturing off the path to protect the natural environment and minimize the risk of encountering dangerous terrain or wildlife.
6. Carry essentials: Pack a backpack with essential items such as a map, compass, flashlight, extra food, and a first aid kit. It's also advisable to bring a fully charged cell phone for emergencies.
7. Monitor weather conditions: Keep an eye on weather forecasts, especially during monsoon season, to avoid being caught in flash floods or severe weather conditions.
8. Hike with a companion: Whenever possible, hike or explore outdoor areas with a companion. This ensures that you have someone to help in emergencies or unexpected situations.

Remember, it's crucial to prioritize your safety when enjoying the outdoors in Phoenix. Use common sense and follow these safety tips for a memorable and safe experience in beautiful natural surroundings.

HIKING

Phoenix, Arizona, offers a plethora of hiking trails for outdoor enthusiasts of all levels. Whether you're a beginner looking for a leisurely stroll or an experienced hiker seeking a challenging adventure, there are trails to suit your preferences.

Camelback Mountain is famous for offering two main trails: Echo Canyon and Cholla. These trails provide stunning city views and a challenging ascent to the summit. Piestewa Peak, another prominent hiking destination, offers multiple trails of varying difficulty levels. The Summit Trail is particularly popular for its steep incline and panoramic views.

For those seeking a more leisurely hike, the Desert Botanical Garden trails showcase the beauty of the Sonoran Desert with interpretive signs highlighting the unique flora and fauna. South Mountain Park, the largest municipal park in the US, offers numerous trails with varying lengths and difficulty levels, allowing hikers to explore its diverse desert landscape.

The McDowell Sonoran Preserve is another remarkable hiking destination, offering an extensive network of trails across thousands of acres of protected land. From easy loops to longer, more challenging treks, the preserve provides ample opportunities to immerse oneself in the stunning Sonoran Desert scenery.

No matter which trail you choose, always remember to hike responsibly, bring plenty of water, wear appropriate attire, and be mindful of the desert environment and wildlife. Go to www.alltrails.com for trail maps and details.

Easy Trails

Double Butte Loop and Hole-in-the-Rock Trail in Papago Park

The Double Butte Loop offers a hike with scenic views of the surrounding desert landscape, including unique rock formations and vegetation. The trail is well-maintained and suitable for hikers of various skill levels. On the other hand, the Hole-in-the-Rock Trail is a short and easy hike leading to a natural rock formation with a hollow opening, providing a picturesque vantage point overlooking the city skyline.

625 N Galvin Pkwy, Phoenix, AZ 85008

Double Butte Loop
 Distance: 2.3 miles (3.7km) Loop
 Elevation Change: 50 feet
 Average Time: 45m

Hole-in-the-Rock Trail

Distance: .16 miles (.26km) Out & Back
Elevation Change: 200 feet
Average Time: 7m

Blevins Trail in Usery Mountain Regional Park

This scenic hiking trail offers a beautiful desert experience. The trail winds through the park's diverse landscape, showcasing stunning views of the surrounding mountains, cacti, and desert flora. With its well-marked path and gradual elevation changes, Blevins Trail is accessible to hikers of various skill levels. Hikers may encounter wildlife such as rabbits, quail, and coyotes along the way. Whether you're seeking a peaceful nature retreat or a refreshing outdoor workout.
3939 N Usery Pass Rd, Mesa, AZ 85207
Distance: 3.1 miles (5km) Loop
Elevation Change: 118 feet
Average Time: 1h 27m

Waterfall Trail in White Tank Mountain Regional Park

This popular hiking trail is known for its stunning desert waterfall during the rainy season. The trail takes hikers on a scenic journey through the rugged desert terrain, offering captivating views of the mountains surrounding you and Phoenix's trademark rock formations. The trail's highlight is the seasonal waterfall, which cascades down the rocks, creating a refreshing oasis in the arid landscape. Hikers can enjoy the tranquility of the desert and the enchanting sight and sound of the waterfall, making the Waterfall Trail a must-visit destination for nature enthusiasts and photographers.
20304 West White Tank Mountain Road, Waddell, AZ 85355
Distance: 1.8 miles (2.9km) Out & Back
Elevation Change: 229 feet
Average Time: 45m

HIKING, CAMPING & OUTDOOR ACTIVITIES

Phoenix South Mountain Loop in South Mountain Preserve

The Phoenix South Mountain Loop is a wheelchair-accessible trail in the South Mountain Preserve, offering a fantastic outdoor experience for individuals with mobility challenges. The paved trail provides stunning views of the desert landscape, encompassing scenic vistas of Phoenix and the surrounding mountains. As a wheelchair-accessible trail, it is designed to accommodate individuals with disabilities, featuring a smooth surface and accessible facilities. Whether you're looking to enjoy a leisurely stroll, soak in the beauty of nature, or capture memorable photographs, the Phoenix South Mountain Loop ensures that everyone can explore and appreciate the natural wonders of the South Mountain Preserve.

10919 S Central Ave, Phoenix, AZ 85042
Distance: 1.3 miles (2.1km)
Elevation Change: 88 feet
Average Time: 27m

Moderate Trails

Hidden Valley Trail via Morman Trail in South Mountain Preserve

These trails are captivating hiking routes in the South Mountain Preserve, Phoenix. It takes hikers through a diverse desert landscape, including rocky terrains, winding canyons, and fascinating geological formations. The trail leads to the Hidden Valley, a secluded and picturesque area nestled between mountain peaks. Hikers will encounter breathtaking panoramic views, unique flora and fauna, and an adventurous experience navigating through narrow passageways.

10919 S Central Ave, Phoenix, AZ 85042
Distance: 3.6 miles (5.8km) Loop
Elevation Change: 925 feet
Average Time: 2h

Pinnacle Peak Trail in Pinnacle Peak Park

The park in Scottsdale, Arizona, is a tourist-attracting hiking destination known for its stunning desert scenery and panoramic views. The trail offers a hike, meandering through rugged desert terrain and granite boulder formations. As hikers ascend the trail, they are rewarded with breathtaking vistas of the surrounding Sonoran Desert and the city below. The Pinnacle Peak Trail showcases the area's natural beauty, featuring diverse plant life, wildlife sightings, and an immersive outdoor experience.

26802 N 102nd Way, Scottsdale, AZ 85262
Distance: 3.8 miles (6.1km) Out & Back
Elevation Change: 1023 feet
Average Time: 2h 10m

Lookout Mountain Summit Trail in Phoenix Mountain Preserve

This trail offers a rewarding hiking experience with panoramic views of the Phoenix metropolitan area. This moderate trail takes hikers on a scenic ascent through desert vegetation and rocky terrain to the summit of Lookout Mountain. Once at the top, visitors are greeted with breathtaking views of the surrounding mountains, city skyline, and stunning sunsets. The trail is well-maintained, providing a challenging yet accessible hike for outdoor enthusiasts.

2701 Piestewa Peak Dr, Phoenix, AZ 85016
Distance: .9 miles (1.4km) Out & Back
Elevation Change: 469 feet
Average Time: 45m

Dixie Mountain Loop in the Phoenix Sonoran Preserve

This captivating trail showcases the beauty of the desert landscape. This moderately challenging Loop takes hikers on a journey through pristine desert terrain, offering panoramic views of the surrounding mountains and valleys. Hikers can appreciate the diverse flora and fauna along the trail, including towering saguaro cacti and desert wildflowers. The Dixie Mountain Loop provides an opportunity to immerse oneself in the tranquility of the Sonoran Desert while enjoying a satisfying hike.

1900 W Desert Vista Trail H 0, Phoenix, AZ 85085

Distance: 4.6 miles (7.4km) Loop

Elevation Change: 741 feet

Average Time: 2h

Difficult Trails

Echo Canyon Trail on Camelback Mountain

The Echo Canyon Trail is a renowned hike for its challenging trail that draws adventurers seeking breathtaking views and a thrilling outdoor experience. Ascending the steep and rocky terrain, hikers navigate through narrow passages and scramble over boulders on their way to the summit. The reward at the top is an awe-inspiring panorama of the Phoenix metropolitan area and the surrounding desert landscape. The Echo Canyon Trail offers a rigorous workout and an opportunity to immerse oneself in the natural beauty of Camelback Mountain. It is popular for those seeking a thrilling adventure and a sense of accomplishment.

E McDonald Dr, Phoenix, AZ 85018

Distance: 2.6 miles (4.2km) Out and Back

Elevation Change: 1522 feet

Average Time: 1h 45m

Tom's Thumb Trail South in the McDowell Sonoran Preserve

Tom's Thumb Trail South offers a remarkable outdoor experience. This trail leads hikers through scenic desert landscapes and fascinating rock formations, with the prominent Tom's Thumb as the highlight. The trail rewards hikers with breathtaking panoramic views of the Sonoran Desert.

It is a favorite among nature enthusiasts, providing to explore the natural wonders of the McDowell Sonoran Preserve while enjoying a satisfying hike. Tom's Thumb Trail South is a must-visit destination for those seeking adventure and stunning vistas in this remarkable desert preserve.

Tom's Thumb Trail, Scottsdale, AZ 85255
Distance: 11.3 miles (18.2km) Out & Back
Elevation Change: 2559 feet
Average Time: 5h 56m

Piestewa Peak Summit Trail #300 in Phoenix Mountain Preserve

This iconic hiking trail within the Phoenix Mountain Preserve ascends to the summit of Piestewa Peak. It offers a rigorous workout and stunning panoramic views of the Phoenix skyline and surrounding mountain ranges. Hikers will encounter steep inclines, rocky terrain, and numerous steps. The reward at the top is an exhilarating sense of accomplishment and breathtaking vistas.

2701 Piestewa Peak Dr, Phoenix, AZ 85016
Distance: 2.3 miles (3.7km) Out & Back
Elevation Change: 1151 feet
Average Time: 1h 30m

Flatiron via Siphon Draw Trail in Lost Dutchman State Park

The Flatiron Trail is a thrilling and strenuous hiking adventure for those seeking a challenge. This iconic trail takes hikers through the picturesque Sonoran Desert, leading to the distinct rock formation known as the Flatiron. With steep ascents, rugged terrain, and occasional scrambling, the trail rewards hikers with breathtaking views of the surrounding Superstition Mountains and the vast desert landscape. The sense of accomplishment upon reaching the Flatiron Summit is unparalleled. The Flatiron via Siphon Draw Trail offers an unforgettable experience for outdoor enthusiasts and seasoned hikers looking to test their skills in the beautiful and rugged Lost

HIKING, CAMPING & OUTDOOR ACTIVITIES

Dutchman State Park.
  6109 Apache Trail, Apache Junction, AZ 85119
  Distance: 5.5 miles (9km) Out & Back
  Elevation Change: 2627 feet
  Average Time: 4h 15m

LAKES

Lake Pleasant Regional Park

Lake Pleasant, located in the northwest Phoenix metropolitan area, is a scenic reservoir offering a wide range of recreational activities. Its expansive water surface and surrounding desert landscape provide a picturesque escape for boating, fishing, swimming, scuba diving, and water sports enthusiasts. The lake's pristine waters and surrounding parkland offer hiking, camping, and picnicking opportunities, making it a popular destination for nature lovers. Lake Pleasant also boasts marinas, boat rentals, and fishing docks, catering to outdoor enthusiasts. Whether you're looking for a day of relaxation by the water or an adventure-filled weekend, Lake Pleasant offers a refreshing retreat from the urban bustle of Phoenix. www.visitpeoriaaz.com is an excellent resource for activities, but below are a couple of highlights.
  41835 N. Castle Hot Springs Road

Activities & Equipment Rentals

Pleasant Harbor Marina

  Here you can find boat, paddleboard, and kayak rentals. American Sailing Association offers sailing lessons and clinics. You can also enjoy Restaurants, yacht training, sightseeing cruises, and the world's largest floating waterslide.
  40202 N 87th Ave Peoria, AZ 85383
  (623) 235-6130

www.pleasantharbor.com

Scorpion Bay Marina

You'll be able to rent various boats, kayaks, water skis, wakeboards, tubes, and jet skis. Scorpion Bay Grille has a diverse menu with stunning water views. Paqua Park is a kid-friendly floating water park for the whole family. Tickets and life jackets are required, so visit the website for details

10970 W. Peninsula Rd. Peoria, AZ 85383

(928) 501 2628

www.scorpionbayaz.com

Saguaro Lake

Saguaro Lake, nestled in the Tonto National Forest near Phoenix, Arizona, is a stunning reservoir that captivates visitors with its scenic beauty. Surrounded by majestic saguaro cacti, rugged mountains, and desert landscapes, the lake offers a tranquil retreat for outdoor enthusiasts. Boating, kayaking, paddleboarding, and horseback riding are popular activities. At the same time, fishing enthusiasts can cast their lines in search of bass and trout. Saguaro Lake's pristine shoreline is also perfect for picnicking, hiking along scenic trails, or simply relaxing and taking in the breathtaking views. With its serene ambiance and natural splendor, Saguaro Lake provides a memorable escape into the heart of the Arizona desert.

12000 N Bush Highway Mesa, AZ 85264

Activities & Equipment Rentals

Saguaro Lake Marina

Rent a Pontoon or take a scenic cruise on the Desert Belle. The Shiprock Restaurant is open for breakfast, lunch, and dinner, so there's no need to pack much. The marina provides visitors with everything they need to enjoy a day on the water surrounded by the beautiful Sonoran Desert.

14011 N Bush Highway, Mesa, AZ 85215

(480) 986-5546
www.saguarolakemarina.com

Saguaro Lake Ranch Stable

Saguaro Lake Ranch Stable offers horseback riding adventures for all experience levels. With scenic trails winding through the stunning Sonoran Desert, visitors can enjoy guided rides, lessons, and even sunset or moonlight rides, immersing themselves in the beauty of the Southwest landscape. The minimum age is 7 years old, and the max weight is 220lbs

13050 N Bush Highway, Mesa, AZ 85215
(480) 984-0335
www.saguarolakeranchstable.com

Canyon Lake

Canyon Lake, located in the Superstition Mountains near Tortilla Flat, Arizona, is a breathtaking reservoir known for its striking beauty and outdoor recreational opportunities. Surrounded by rugged cliffs and towering canyons, the lake offers a picturesque setting for boating, fishing, kayaking, and paddleboarding. The tranquil waters teem with various fish species, attracting anglers from near and far. Scenic hiking trails around the lake allow nature enthusiasts to explore the desert landscape and enjoy stunning vistas. Whether you're seeking a day of relaxation or an adventure-filled outing, Canyon Lake offers a serene escape in the midst of Arizona's natural wonders.

5140 East Ingram Street, Mesa, AZ 85205

Activities & Equipment Rentals

The Dolly Steamboat Cruise and Tour

The Dolly Steamboat Tours offer a unique experience in Arizona's Superstition Mountains, from the Scenic Nature Tour to the Twilight Dinner Cruise Cruise. Cruising along the tranquil waters of Canyon Lake, visitors can enjoy narrated tours, wildlife sightings, and breathtaking views of the surrounding cliffs and desert landscape.

16802 AZ-88, Tortilla Flat, AZ 85117

(480) 827-9144

https://dollysteamboat.com

Canyon Lake Marina and Campground

The marina provides boat rentals, fishing supplies, and a launch ramp for water activities, while the campground offers scenic campsites for overnight stays. With access to hiking trails, fishing spots, and stunning lake views, Canyon Lake Marina and Campground is ideal for nature lovers who want to avoid fighting the crowds.

16802 AZ-88, Apache Junction, AZ 85119

(480) 288-9233

www.canyonlakemarina.com

Apache Lake

Apache Lake, located along the Apache Trail in Arizona, is a hidden gem nestled amidst the rugged Superstition Mountains and Tonto National Forest. This picturesque reservoir offers a serene and unspoiled setting for outdoor enthusiasts. Boating, fishing, kayaking, and water sports are popular activities on the calm waters of Apache Lake, known for its abundant bass and trout. The surrounding desert landscape provides ample hiking, camping, and wildlife-spotting opportunities. With its remote location and breathtaking vistas, Apache Lake offers a tranquil escape from bustling city life and a chance to connect with nature. This is a long drive from Phoenix's center, so consider planning an overnight trip.

The best directions to the lake are found here: https://apachelake.com/directions-apache-lake/

Activities & Equipment Rentals

The Apache Lake Marina and Resort

The Apache Lake Marina and Resort, situated on the scenic Apache Lake in Arizona, offers a variety of amenities and services for visitors. With a marina providing boat rentals, a lakeside restaurant, RV camping facilities, and comfortable accommodations, it is a perfect base for enjoying water activities, exploring the natural beauty, and experiencing a relaxing getaway amid the picturesque desert landscape.

229.5 Mile Marker, Roosevelt, AZ 85545

(928) 923-6690

www.apachelake.com

Roosevelt Lake

Roosevelt Lake, located in central Arizona, has a rich history that dates back to the early 20th century. The lake's creation was part of a larger water management project known as the Salt River Project, designed to harness water from the Salt River for irrigation and power generation. Construction of the Roosevelt Dam began in 1903. It was completed in 1911, making it one of the largest masonry dams in the world at the time. The dam was named in honor of President Theodore Roosevelt, who played a significant role in promoting conservation and water management efforts.

As the state's largest lake by surface area, it offers a wealth of recreational activities and scenic beauty. The crystal-clear waters of Roosevelt Lake are a haven for boating, fishing, water skiing, and kayaking, attracting outdoor enthusiasts from near and far. Anglers can cast their lines for bass, crappie, and catfish. The lake is also famous for camping, picnicking, and wildlife spotting. The landscape is surrounded by rolling hills and majestic saguaro cacti and provides a picturesque backdrop for outdoor adventures. Remember to explore the Visitors Center created in honor of this historic spot.

Activities & Equipment Rentals

Roosevelt Lake Visitors Center

Located near the dam, it offers information about the lake's construction, water management, and recreational opportunities. Visitors can learn about the area's cultural heritage and enjoy panoramic views of the reservoir.

(602) 225-5395

www.discovergilacounty.com/roosevelt-lake-attractions

Tonto National Monument

This fascinating archaeological site preserves ancient cliff dwellings and artifacts. The monument consists of two well-preserved Pueblo ruins, the Lower Cliff Dwelling and the Upper Cliff Dwelling, inhabited by the Salado culture over 700 years ago. Visitors can embark on guided tours to explore the remarkable cliff dwellings, marvel at the intricate architecture, and learn about the lives of the people who once called this place home. The monument also offers hiking trails with stunning views of the surrounding Sonoran Desert and the Tonto Basin. Tonto National Monument is a remarkable destination for history enthusiasts and those seeking a deeper understanding of Arizona's rich Native American heritage.

26260 AZ-188, Roosevelt, AZ 85545

www.discovergilacounty.com/tonto-national-moument

CAMPING

Camping in Phoenix, Arizona, offers outdoor enthusiasts a chance to immerse themselves in the stunning desert landscape while enjoying a range of recreational activities. Several campgrounds and camping areas in and around Phoenix cater to different preferences and needs.

One popular camping spot is McDowell Mountain Regional Park, located northeast of Phoenix. It offers well-maintained campgrounds with various amenities, including water and electric hookups, restrooms, and showers. The park also features hiking and mountain biking trails, making it an ideal choice for outdoor adventurers.

When camping in Phoenix, preparing for the desert environment is essential. Carry plenty of water, sunscreen, and appropriate clothing to protect against the sun and heat. Follow fire regulations and be mindful of wildlife.

Overall, camping in Phoenix provides a chance to connect with nature and enjoy the unique beauty of the desert landscape, all while being within reach of the city's amenities and attractions. Whether you prefer a developed campground or a more primitive camping experience, there are options to suit every camper's preferences in the Phoenix area.

Estrella Mountain Regional Park

Estrella Mountain Regional Park is located southwest of Phoenix, Arizona. It offers camping opportunities in a scenic desert setting and educational programs to engage the whole family. See the website for the calendar of events. The park features well-maintained campgrounds with amenities such as restrooms, showers, picnic tables, and fire pits. Visitors can enjoy hiking and biking trails, wildlife viewing, and stargazing. The peaceful surroundings and beautiful mountain views make Estrella Mountain Regional Park a popular destination for camping and outdoor recreation in the Phoenix area.

14805 W. Vineyard Ave. Goodyear, AZ 85338
(602) 506-2930 ext. 6
Reservation Fees: $15-$40
www.maricopacountyparks.net/park-locator/estrella-mountain-regional-park/

Lost Dutchman State Park

Camping in Lost Dutchman State Park is an unforgettable experience for nature enthusiasts. Nestled in the Sonoran Desert near Apache Junction, Arizona, the park offers campsites with stunning views of the legendary Superstition Mountains. Campers can immerse themselves in the serene desert landscape, enjoying the tranquility and starry nights. The park provides well-maintained facilities, including picnic areas, restrooms, and showers. With numerous hiking trails, including the famous Siphon Draw Trail leading to the Flatiron, camping in Lost Dutchman State Park offers endless opportunities for exploration and adventure. It also incorporates technology to enhance your hiking experience with Geocaching and Earthcatching. Visit the website for details.

6109 N. Apache Trail, Apache Junction, AZ 85119
(480) 982-4485
Reservation Fees: $20-$35
www.azstateparks.com/lost-dutchman

Lake Pleasant Regional Park

The park provides various camping options, including developed campgrounds and primitive sites. Campers can enjoy beautiful lake views, surrounding mountains, and desert landscapes. The park offers picnic tables, fire rings, restrooms, and showers. Outdoor enthusiasts can indulge in boating, fishing, kayaking, and hiking, with numerous trails available. The tranquil ambiance, starry nights, and proximity to water activities make camping in Lake Pleasant Regional Park a popular choice for nature lovers and those seeking a peaceful retreat in the picturesque Arizona desert. See some highlighted activities in the Lakes section of this book.

41835 N. Castle Hot Springs Rd. Morristown, AZ 85342
(602) 506-2930 ext. 2
Reservation Fees: $15-$40
www.maricopacountyparks.net/park-locator/lake-pleasant-regional-park

White Tank Mountain Regional Park

This park offers camping opportunities amidst the stunning desert landscape. Campers can choose from spacious campsites equipped with picnic tables and fire rings, perfect for a relaxing getaway. The park features miles of scenic hiking trails, allowing visitors to explore the rugged beauty of the White Tank Mountains. Nature lovers can enjoy wildlife spotting, stargazing, and breathtaking views of the Sonoran Desert. With modern amenities like restrooms and showers, camping in White Tank Mountain Regional Park offers a peaceful retreat and a chance to reconnect with nature just a short drive from the bustling city. Some programs have limited participation reservations available, so planning ahead is highly recommended.

20304 W. White Tank Mountain Road Waddell, AZ 85355

(602) 506-2930 ext. 5

Reservation Fees: $15-$40

www.maricopacountyparks.net/park-locator/white-tank-mountain-regional-park

McDowell Mountain Regional Park

Camping in McDowell Mountain Regional Park is a remarkable outdoor experience for nature enthusiasts. Located northeast of Phoenix, Arizona, the park offers well-maintained campgrounds with amenities, including electric hookups, restrooms, and showers. Campers can immerse themselves in the serene desert surroundings, surrounded by the picturesque McDowell Mountains. The park boasts an extensive network of horseback riding, biking, and hiking trails, allowing visitors to explore the diverse flora and fauna of the Sonoran Desert. With stunning mountain vistas, peaceful campsites, and a variety of outdoor activities, camping in McDowell Mountain Regional Park is an ideal getaway for those seeking tranquility and adventure in the Arizona desert.

16300 McDowell Mountain Park Dr. Fountain Hills, AZ 85268

(602) 506-2930 ext 3

Reservation Fees: $15-$40

www.maricopacountyparks.net/mcdowell-mountain-regional-park

4

Activities

NIGHTLIFE

Phoenix, Arizona, offers a vibrant and diverse nightlife scene that caters to various tastes and preferences. There is something for everyone, from trendy bars and nightclubs to live music venues and cultural experiences.

Downtown Phoenix is a hub of activity, particularly along Roosevelt Row and in the Roosevelt Arts District. Here, you'll find a mix of stylish cocktail lounges, craft beer bars, and trendy nightclubs. The area comes alive with live music performances, art exhibits, and cultural events detailed in Chapter 2 of this book.

Also, in Chapter 2, Scottsdale's Old Town is another popular destination for nightlife. The district is known for its upscale bars, stylish lounges, and trendy nightclubs. Visitors can enjoy a night of dancing, live music, or sipping handcrafted cocktails in a chic environment.

If you're a fan of live music, Phoenix has a thriving music scene. The Crescent Ballroom, Valley Bar, and The Van Buren are just a few of the venues that showcase local and touring artists across various genres. Whether you're into rock, jazz, hip-hop, or indie music, there are plenty of options to catch a memorable live performance.

Overall, the nightlife in Phoenix is diverse and vibrant, catering to various interests and preferences. Whether you're looking for a laid-back evening at a cozy bar, an energetic night of dancing, or a cultural experience, Phoenix has a multitude of options to keep you entertained well into the night. Below are some top spots to dance the night away.

Monarch Theatre

This multi-level theatre in downtown Phoenix is famous for its live music and electronic music scene. With its industrial-chic decor, state-of-the-art sound system, and renowned DJs, the venue offers an immersive experience for electronic music lovers and party-goers.
   122 E Washington St, Phoenix, AZ 85004
   (602) 821-8569
   www.monarchtheatre.com

Crescent Ballroom

Also, in downtown Phoenix, this music venue showcases a diverse range of live performances, complete with creative theme nights to keep every visit bursting with new experiences. It's an intimate setting with stellar sound quality and excellent food and drinks.
   308 N 2nd Ave, Phoenix, AZ 85003
   (602) 716-2222
   www.crescentphx.com

Dwntwn

Considered Arizona's #1 Latin Dance Club, Dwntwn touts 3 different rooms, each with its own bar and a different music and dancing genre. The energy vibrates in every room of this club, and the music will have you dancing with or without liquid courage.
   702 N Central Ave, Phoenix, AZ 85004
   www.clubdwntwn.com

Charlie's

Charlie's in Phoenix is a popular LGBTQ+ nightclub and entertainment venue that has been a staple in the local community for decades. Known for its drag shows, and themed parties, Charlie's offers a welcoming and inclusive space for all. Its energetic dance floor, friendly staff, and vibrant events make it a must-visit destination.

727 W Camelback Rd, Phoenix, AZ 85013
(602) 265-0224
www.charliesphoenix.com

Tru Ultra Lounge

A premier hip-hop club that caters to music enthusiasts seeking an unforgettable night out. Tru Ultra Lounge creates a dynamic space for hip-hop lovers to dance, socialize, and enjoy the latest beats in a stylish setting.

915 N. Central Ave. Phoenix, AZ 85004
(602) 367-0607
www.truultralounge.com

Rip's Bar

RIP's Bar in Phoenix is a beloved neighborhood dive bar serving the local community for years. With its laid-back and friendly atmosphere, Rip's Bar offers a casual spot to unwind, enjoy a cold drink, and catch up with friends. Its unpretentious vibe and affordable prices make it a welcome change of pace from other nightclubs around town.

3045 N 16th St, Phoenix, AZ 85016
(602) 266-0015
www.ripsbar.weebly.com

Scootin' Boots Dance Hall

If country music and line dancing are your thing, then Scootin' Boots Dance Hall is your destination. It offers a spacious dance floor, live music performances, and an energetic crowd for your favorite Country and Western dancing genre.

   515 N Stapley Dr #103, Mesa, AZ 85203

   (480) 450-1432

   www.scootinbootsdancehallmesa.com

AQUARIUMS & ZOOS

Phoenix, Arizona, is home to several outstanding aquariums and zoos that allow visitors to explore and learn about diverse animal species worldwide.

One of the most notable attractions is the OdySea Aquarium in Scottsdale. Spanning over 200,000 square feet, it is the largest aquarium in the Southwest. Another prominent destination is the Phoenix Zoo, one of the largest non-profit zoos in the United States.

The Phoenix Herpetological Society is a must-visit for those interested in exotic reptiles. It is a non-profit organization that rescues and rehabilitates reptiles and amphibians, showcasing a vast collection of species from around the globe.

Furthermore, the Wildlife World Zoo, Aquarium & Safari Park, located in Litchfield Park, provides a unique experience by combining a zoo, aquarium, and safari park in one place.

Phoenix's aquariums and zoos offer fascinating opportunities to connect with wildlife, explore different ecosystems, and learn about conservation efforts.

Out of Africa Wildlife Park

This captivating destination offers visitors an up-close encounter with exotic animals from around the world. This unique wildlife park provides interactive experiences, thrilling safari tours, and educational shows.

   3505 AZ-260, Camp Verde, AZ 86322

(928) 567-2840

Tickets: Children under 3 are free; Others range from $27.95-$42.95. See the website for additional attractions to customize your experience.

www.outofafricapark.com

Bearzona Wildlife Park

For a unique experience, this park combines a drive-through wildlife experience with a walk-through area. Visitors can drive through the park and observe North American animals such as bears, bison, and wolves. The walk-through area offers an opportunity to see smaller animals up close and enjoy interactive exhibits.

1500 E Rte 66, Williams, AZ 86046

(928) 635-2289

Tickets: Children under 3 are free; Others range from $20-$35

www.bearizona.com

OdySea Aquarium

This Aquarium features interactive exhibits, touch pools, and informative presentations, allowing visitors to get close to marine life, including sharks, sea turtles, and penguins. The aquarium also houses a 3D theater and hosts educational programs and events.

9500 East Vía de Ventura Suite A-100, Scottsdale, AZ 85256

(480) 291-8000

Tickets: Children under 2 are free; Others range from $34.95-$44.95. See the website for a customizable experience.

www.odyseaaquarium.com

Phoenix Zoo

The zoo is dedicated to conservation and hosts over 3,000 animals from various habitats. Visitors can encounter endangered species such as orangutans, Sumatran tigers, and African elephants. The zoo offers educational exhibits, a children's trail, and interactive experiences like giraffe feeding. It also participates in wildlife conservation initiatives worldwide.

455 N Galvin Pkwy, Phoenix, AZ 85008

(602) 286-3800

Tickets: Children under 3 are free; Others range from $27.95-$39.95 (Discounts when purchased online)

www.phoenixzoo.org

Sea Life Arizona

Located in Tempe, this immersive aquarium experience transports visitors into an underwater world. With a diverse selection of exhibits and interactive displays, guests can get up close to fascinating marine creatures, including sharks, rays, seahorses, and more. Educational presentations and feeding demonstrations make Sea Life Arizona a fun and educational outing for all ages.

5000 S Arizona Mills Cir Suite 145, Tempe, AZ 85282

(480) 565-7072

Tickets: Children 3 and under are free; Others start at $16.99. The website says prices are subject to change, so plan ahead.

www.visitsealife.com/arizona

Wildlife World Zoo & Aquarium

Wildlife World Zoo is an expansive facility with interactive experiences like feeding shows and a safari park. It houses diverse animals, from lions and tigers to giraffes and zebras. The aquarium features marine life, including sharks, sea turtles, and colorful tropical fish.

16501 W Northern Ave, Litchfield Park, AZ 85340

(623) 935-9453

Tickets: Children under 3 are free; Others range from $25.50-$45.50

www.wildlifeworld.com

KID-FRIENDLY

i.d.e.a. Museum

i.d.e.a. Museum in Phoenix is a creative and interactive museum designed for children and families. With its hands-on exhibits, art installations, and engaging activities, the museum fosters imagination, learning, and creativity. From art studios to sensory experiences, I.D.E.A. Museum offers a fun and educational environment for children to explore and express their inner artists.

150 W Pepper Pl, Mesa, AZ 85201
(480) 644-2468
Tickets: Children under 1 are free; Others are $9
www.ideamuseum.org

Golfland Sunsplash

Welcome to a popular family entertainment center that offers a mix of mini-golf, water slides, and arcade games in Mesa, AZ. You'll also enjoy go-carts, bumper cars, bumper boats, and what kid-friendly space is complete without Pizza!

155 W Hampton Ave, Mesa, AZ 85210
(480) 834-8319
Tickets: Each activity is priced either a la carte or in a combination of packages. Children under 1 are free, and children between 1-3 are discounted to $5.99
www.golfland.com/mesa

Butterfly Wonderland

Discover a magical indoor rainforest habitat that showcases thousands of butterflies from around the world. Visitors can walk through the lush tropical garden and witness the beauty and grace of these delicate creatures up close. With interactive exhibits and educational programs, Butterfly Wonderland offers a captivating experience for all ages.

9500 East Vía de Ventura F100, Scottsdale, AZ 85256

(480) 800-3000

Tickets: Children under 2 are free; Others range from $19.95-$29.95; packages to bundle other attractions are available on the website.

www.butterflywonderland.com

Crayola Experience

Unleash the kids for an imaginative and colorful attraction where they can explore their creativity. With interactive exhibits, hands-on activities, and a wide array of Crayola-themed experiences, children can immerse themselves in a world of art and imagination. From creating their own crayon labels to participating in crafts and interactive shows, Crayola Experience offers a vibrant and engaging adventure for young artists.

3111 W Chandler Blvd Suite 2154, Chandler, AZ 85226

(602) 581-5370

Tickets: Children under 3 are free: Others range from $21.99-$24.99 (Discount if you buy online)

www.crayolaexperience.com/chandler

Gold Field Ghost Town & Mine Tours

Take the kids back in time to this historical attraction that takes visitors to the Wild West era. The ghost town is filled with old buildings, exhibits, and artifacts that recreate the atmosphere of a bygone era. Guests can explore the old mine, go horseback riding, fly down a zip line, enjoy a gunfighter's show, and even try their hand at panning for gold. It's a unique and immersive experience that offers a glimpse into Arizona's rich mining history.

4650 N Mammoth Mine Rd, Apache Junction, AZ 85119

(480) 983-0333

Tickets: Each attraction is sold a la cart; see website for details www.goldfieldghosttown.com

McCormick-Stillman Railroad Park

Chug down the track to Scottsdale for this delightful destination for train enthusiasts of all ages. The park features a meticulously restored vintage railroad with a train ride that winds through beautiful surroundings. Visitors can explore the museum, ride a carousel, and enjoy the expansive playgrounds. It's a charming and nostalgic experience for the whole family.

7301 E Indian Bend Rd, Scottsdale, AZ 85250

(480) 312-2312

Tickets: Some attractions are free for all ages, while others have minimal ticket prices. See website for details. The schedule changes month to month, so planning ahead is highly recommended.

www.therailroadpark.com

THEME PARKS & WATER PARKS

Lego Land Discovery Center

Escape the summer heat to this ultimate indoor playground and educational experience for LEGO enthusiasts. With a range of LEGO-themed attractions, including rides, interactive exhibits, and building stations, kids can immerse themselves in a world of creativity and fun. It's a perfect destination for LEGO fans to explore, build, and play to their heart's content.

5000 S Arizona Mills Cir STE 135, Tempe, AZ 85282

(480) 565-7072

Tickets: Children under 3 are free; Others start at $25.99. Packages for additional attractions are available. An adult must accompany children under 12, and adults must be accompanied with a minor.

www.legolanddiscoverycenter.com/arizona

Six Flags Hurricane Harbor

A summer staple is a trip to this thrilling water park that offers an escape from the desert heat. Various water slides, wave pools, lazy rivers, and splash zones provide endless opportunities for fun and relaxation. From adrenaline-pumping rides to family-friendly attractions, Hurricane Harbor offers a refreshing and exciting aquatic adventure for all ages.

   4243 W Pinnacle Peak Rd, Glendale, AZ 85310

   (623) 201-2000

   Tickets: Starting at $30 with multiple bundle options

   www.sixflags.com

Great Wolf Lodge

This family-friendly resort and water park offers a memorable getaway for all ages. With its indoor water park featuring thrilling slides, lazy rivers, splash zones, and other amenities like themed rooms, interactive games, and dining options, Great Wolf Lodge provides year-round family memories!

   7333 N Pima Rd, Scottsdale, AZ 85258

   (480) 948-9653

   Tickets: Half-day passes start at $63, full day start at $70. Packages available.

   www.greatwolf.com

Enchanted Island Amusement Park

Be enchanted by this charming, family-friendly destination that offers classic amusement park fun with various rides, including carousels, trains, boats, and a splash zone. Enchanted Island feels like a themed carnival that decided to stay forever!

   1202 W Encanto Blvd, Phoenix, AZ 85007

   (602) 254-1200

   Tickets: Admission to the park is free; pay per ride as you would at a carnival, starting at $5.50.

   www.enchantedisland.com

BOTANICAL GARDENS

Phoenix, Arizona, is home to several exquisite botanical gardens that showcase the region's diverse plant life and offer a serene escape into nature. These gardens provide a perfect setting for leisurely walks, educational experiences, and appreciating the natural beauty of the desert.

The Desert Botanical Garden in Papago Park is a must-visit destination. Spread across 140 acres, it features an impressive collection of desert plants worldwide. The Japanese Friendship Garden, known as Ro Ho En, is a tranquil oasis in downtown Phoenix. And

The Boyce Thompson Arboretum, located east of Phoenix, is a sprawling botanical garden featuring over 3,000 species of desert plants from around the world.

Each botanical garden in Phoenix provides a unique experience, highlighting the region's distinctive flora and offering a peaceful respite from the city. These gardens showcase the beauty of desert landscapes and play a crucial role in conservation efforts and educating the public about the importance of preserving our natural environment.

Desert Botanical Garden

This garden is a captivating destination that celebrates the remarkable diversity of desert plants. As prompted above, The Desert Botanical Garden is spread across 140 acres; it showcases a stunning collection of cacti, succulents, and wildflowers worldwide. Visitors can wander through beautifully curated gardens, hike along scenic trails, and learn about the fascinating adaptations of desert plants. The garden also hosts seasonal events, art installations, and educational programs highlighting the importance of desert conservation.

1201 N Galvin Pkwy, Phoenix, AZ 85008

(480) 941-1225

Tickets: Children under 2 and Active Duty Military are free; Others range from $14.95-$29.95. Tickets must be purchased in advance.

www.dbg.org

Japanese Friendship Garden

The Japanese Friendship Garden, also known as Ro Ho En, is a serene oasis nestled in downtown Phoenix. Inspired by traditional Japanese gardens, it provides a peaceful retreat for visitors seeking tranquility and beauty. The garden features meticulously designed landscapes, flowing streams, vibrant foliage, and serene koi ponds. Visitors can stroll along the winding paths, cross elegant bridges, and find serenity in the peaceful surroundings. The garden also hosts cultural events, tea ceremonies, and educational programs that allow visitors to immerse themselves in Japanese culture. The Japanese Friendship Garden is a cherished symbol of friendship and a place of harmony where visitors can solace and appreciate nature's beauty.

1125 N 3rd Ave, Phoenix, AZ 85003

(602) 274-8700

Tickets: Children under 6 are free; Others range from $7-$10

www.japanesefriendshipgarden.org

Boyce Thompson Arboretum

Located east of Phoenix, this is an exquisite destination for nature lovers and plant enthusiasts. Spanning over 300 acres, it showcases an impressive collection of desert plants from all over the world. Visitors can wander through diverse landscapes, including lush forests, colorful gardens, and tranquil creeks. The arboretum offers scenic trails that lead to breathtaking vistas, and educational signs provide fascinating insights into the plants and their adaptations. With its rich botanical diversity, guided tours, and educational programs, Boyce Thompson Arboretum is a haven for learning, exploring, and appreciating the natural world.

37615 E Arboretum Way, Superior, AZ 85173

(520) 689-2723

Tickets: Children under 5 are free; Others range from $10-$24.95

www.btarboretum.org

USS Arizona Memorial Gardens at Salt River

The newest of the gardens mentioned in this chapter, the USS Arizona Memorial Gardens, honors the brave soldiers that served at Pearl Harbor on December 7th, 1941. The grounds are now home to the salvaged remains of the battleship that was attacked in Hawaii and offer a place to learn about an integral part of our American history and the men and women that served aboard our namesake ship.

7455 N Pima Rd, Scottsdale, AZ 85258

(480) 362-2700

Tickets are free but plan ahead to make sure the Boat House Relic Room is open.

www.discoversaltriver.com/uss-arizona-memorial-gardens-at-salt-river

ADVENTURING

Rock Climbing

Arizona Climbing Guides is a premier rock climbing guide service that offers thrilling and safe climbing experiences for enthusiasts of all skill levels. Based in Phoenix, Arizona, they specialize in guiding climbers through the stunning and diverse landscapes of the state, including iconic destinations such as Camelback Mountain, McDowell Mountains, and Sedona.

Experienced and certified guides lead climbers on personalized adventures, providing expert instruction, equipment, and support. Whether you're a beginner looking to try climbing for the first time or an experienced climber seeking new challenges, Arizona Climbing Guides offers tailored experiences to meet your goals and abilities.

The guides prioritize safety and adhere to industry-standard practices, ensuring climbers enjoy the experience with peace of mind. They also emphasize environmental stewardship, promoting Leave No Trace principles to minimize the impact on the natural surroundings.

In addition to rock climbing, Arizona Climbing Guides also offers guided canyoneering and rappelling adventures. These unique experiences take participants through stunning slot canyons, offering a thrilling mix of climbing, rappelling, and exploration.

With their extensive knowledge of Arizona's climbing areas and dedication to customer satisfaction, Arizona Climbing Guides provides unforgettable adventures that allow participants to push their boundaries, gain new skills, and experience the beauty of the desert landscape in a unique and exhilarating way.

(520) 829-2200

www.climbingguidesarizona.com

Hot Air Ballooning

Rainbow Ryders Hot Air Balloon Co.

Rainbow Ryders Hot Air Balloon Co. is a renowned hot air balloon company in Phoenix, offering thrilling and memorable adventures in the sky. With a team of experienced pilots and a fleet of colorful balloons, they provide safe and exciting hot-air balloon rides for individuals and groups. Passengers can soar above the picturesque desert landscapes, taking in panoramic views of the Phoenix area. Rainbow Ryders Hot Air Balloon Co. prioritizes customer safety and satisfaction, ensuring a memorable and enchanting experience for all who embark on their balloon flights.

715 E Covey Ln #100, Phoenix, AZ 85024

(480) 299-0154

www.rainbowryders.com/locations/phoenix

Hot Air Expeditions

Hot Air Expeditions is a premier hot air balloon company in Phoenix.

With their skilled pilots and luxurious balloons, they offer unforgettable adventures in the sky. Passengers can experience the beauty of the Sonoran Desert from a unique perspective as they soar gently through the air. Hot Air Expeditions provides personalized and intimate flights, ensuring an exclusive and magical experience. Their attention to safety, exceptional customer service, and dedication to creating lasting memories make Hot Air Expeditions a top choice for those seeking an extraordinary hot-air balloon adventure in Phoenix.

702 W Deer Valley Rd, Phoenix, AZ 85027
(480) 502-6999
www.hotairexpeditions.com

ATV Rentals

Arizona Outdoor Fun Adventures & Tours

This outdoor adventure company offers a wide range of thrilling activities and guided tours that allow visitors to explore the region's stunning landscapes. From exhilarating ATV rides through the Sonoran Desert to scenic jet ski tours on beautiful lakes, Arizona Outdoor Fun provides adrenaline-pumping experiences for adventure enthusiasts. Their experienced guides ensure safety while providing informative commentary about the area's history, geology, and wildlife.

61112 Black Canyon Fwy, New River, AZ 85087
(602) 400-2445
www.azoutdoorfun.com

Extreme Arizona ATV & Jet Ski Rentals

They offer off-road ATV rides and thrilling jet ski adventures for adrenaline junkies. Whether exploring the desert trails on an ATV or gliding across the sparkling waters on a jet ski, Extreme Arizona provides high-quality equipment and safety gear to ensure an exciting and safe experience. With knowledgeable staff, flexible rental options, and well-maintained vehicles, Extreme Arizona ATV & Jet Ski Rentals offers the perfect opportunity to explore the rugged beauty of Arizona's landscapes and create lasting memories of adventure.

  6921 E Cave Creek Rd, Cave Creek, AZ 85331

  (480) 690-9956

  www.extremearizona.com

Time to Ride AZ

Calling all motorcycle enthusiasts and adventurers. Time to Ride AZ offers a wide selection of well-maintained motorcycles, ranging from cruisers to sport bikes, allowing riders to experience the thrill of the open road. Time to Ride AZ provides short-term or longer-term exploration opportunities with flexible rental options, including daily and weekly rates. Their friendly and knowledgeable staff ensures a seamless rental experience, providing safety equipment and tips for a safe and enjoyable ride. Whether you're a local rider or visiting Phoenix, Time to Ride AZ offers the freedom and excitement of motorcycle travel in the stunning landscapes of Arizona.

  7171 E Cave Creek Rd ste J Cave Creek, AZ 85331

  (480) 597-7559

  www.timetorideaz.com

SHOPPING

Phoenix, Arizona, is a shopper's paradise, offering diverse shopping experiences to suit all tastes and preferences. From upscale malls to charming boutiques and unique local markets, there's something for everyone in this vibrant city.

One of the top shopping destinations in Phoenix is Scottsdale Fashion Square, one of the largest luxury malls in the Southwest. It features an impressive selection of high-end brands, designer stores, and upscale boutiques, making it a haven for fashion enthusiasts. The details for this shopping experience are in the Old Town Scottsdale Section of this book.

The Melrose District in central Phoenix is a must-visit for those seeking a more unique and eclectic shopping experience. This trendy neighborhood is filled with vintage shops, retro boutiques, and quirky thrift stores, offering a treasure trove of one-of-a-kind finds.

Another popular shopping spot is Biltmore Fashion Park, an outdoor mall known for its elegant ambiance and upscale retailers. Its lush landscaping and luxurious stores provide a sophisticated shopping experience.

For a taste of local flair, the Phoenix Public Market in downtown Phoenix offers a bustling farmer's market experience where visitors can find fresh produce, artisanal products, and unique crafts from local vendors.

If you're looking for Native American arts and crafts, the Heard Museum Shop showcases a stunning collection of jewelry, pottery, textiles, and artwork made by Native American artists. Find the details to shop here in the Museums section of this book.

The Arizona Mills Mall is also a shopper's paradise with a mix of outlet stores, discount retailers, and entertainment options like an aquarium and an IMAX theater.

Whether you're searching for high-end fashion, vintage gems, local crafts, or bargain deals, Phoenix offers a variety of shopping experiences that cater to every style and budget.

Locally Owned

Frances

Located in Phoenix, this boutique is a beloved local gem that offers a curated collection of unique and artisanal goods. With a focus on supporting independent designers and artists, Frances showcases an array of handmade jewelry, clothing, accessories, and home decor items. This charming boutique provides a warm and inviting atmosphere, making shopping a delightful experience. From trendy fashion pieces to locally crafted treasures, Frances offers a diverse range of products that embody the spirit

of Phoenix's vibrant creative community.
   10 W Camelback Rd STE A, Phoenix, AZ 85013
   (602) 279-5467
   Hours: Monday-Saturday 10am-6pm; Sunday 12pm-5pm
   www.shopfrancesboutique.com

Time Bomb Vintage Clothing

Also in Phoenix, this vintage clothing store takes customers on a nostalgic journey through fashion history. With a carefully curated selection of retro apparel, accessories, and collectibles, Time Bomb Vintage offers unique and one-of-a-kind pieces that capture the essence of bygone eras. From vintage band tees and iconic denim to elegant dresses and statement accessories, this boutique caters to fashion enthusiasts seeking to express their individuality through timeless style. With its welcoming atmosphere and knowledgeable staff, Time Bomb Vintage is a must-visit destination for vintage lovers and those looking to add a touch of nostalgia to their wardrobe.
   4632 N 7th Ave, Phoenix, AZ 85013
   (509) 220-9162
   Hours: Monday-Wednesday Closed; Thursday-Sunday 11am-4:30pm
   www.time-bomb-vintage-clothing.business.site

Changing Hands Bookstore

This iconic independent bookstore has become a beloved cultural hub with 2 locations, one in Phoenix and another in Tempe. With its vast selection of new and used books across various genres and an array of literary events and workshops, Changing Hands Bookstore offers a haven for bookworms and literary enthusiasts. The store's cozy and inviting atmosphere, knowledgeable staff, and commitment to community engagement make it a go-to destination for book lovers, authors, and readers of all ages. Whether you're searching for a new release, a hidden gem, or simply a space to immerse yourself in the world of literature, Changing

Hands Bookstore is a must-visit.

300 W Camelback Rd, Phoenix, AZ 85013

(602) 274-0067

6428 S McClintock Dr, Tempe, AZ 85283

(480) 730-0205

Hours: Monday-Sunday, 10am-8pm

www.changinghands.com

Arizona Hiking Shack

This shop is a go-to destination for outdoor enthusiasts and hikers. This specialty store offers a wide range of gear, equipment, and apparel tailored for hiking and other outdoor activities. Arizona Hiking Shack provides everything you need to embark on your next adventure, from hiking boots and backpacks to camping gear and trail maps. With a knowledgeable staff passionate about hiking and the outdoors, the store offers personalized recommendations and expert advice. Whether you're a beginner or an experienced hiker, Arizona Hiking Shack is a trusted resource for all your hiking needs in the Phoenix area.

3244 E Thomas Rd, Phoenix, AZ 85018

(602) 944-7723

Hours: Monday-Friday 10am-7pm; Saturday 9am-5pm; Sunday 11am-4pm

www.hikingshack.com

Michael Todd's Treasures

This charming shop describes itself as Vintage Home Decor. You'll find furniture, accessories, clothing, and art that are all one of a kind to fit perfectly into your unique space. Come ready to explore because you'll find everything from authentic antiques to that nostalgic knick-knack from childhood. Michael Todd has curated a unique shopping experience you don't want to miss.

ACTIVITIES

4701 N 7th Ave, Phoenix, AZ 85013
(480) 766-9360
Hours: Monday-Tuesday Closed; Wednesday-Friday 11am-4pm; Saturday 10am-5pm; Sunday 11am-4pm
www.facebook.com/profile.php?id=100058823780052

For The People

This incredible shop has curated top-of-the-line home furnishings and art, seamlessly integrating southwestern flare with a modern touch. Enjoy a cup of artisan coffee at the shop, and browse some top local artists to accent your home from your trip, or order that perfect sofa you've been searching for. For the People even offers custom design services to help translate the store's atmosphere to your home.
5102 N Central Ave #5, Phoenix, AZ 85012
(602) 954-4009
Hours: Monday-Saturday 10am-6pm; Sunday 11am-5pm
forthepeoplestore.com

/Now or Never

Now or Never shop in Phoenix is a trendy and curated boutique that offers a unique selection of clothing, accessories, and lifestyle products. With its carefully selected inventory, the shop caters to fashion-forward individuals seeking stylish and one-of-a-kind pieces. From on-trend clothing and statement accessories to home decor and gift items, Now or Never provides a cultivated range of products that capture the essence of contemporary style. With its inviting atmosphere and friendly staff, the shop offers a personalized shopping experience. It is a go-to destination for those looking to stay ahead of the fashion curve in Phoenix.
1001 N Central Ave Suite 100, Phoenix, AZ 85004
(480) 676-0076
Hours: Monday-Saturday 11am-6pm; Sunday 12pm-5pm

www.nowornever.shop

Farmers Markets

Phoenix is home to a vibrant and thriving farmers market scene, where locals and visitors can immerse themselves in a cornucopia of fresh produce, artisanal products, and community vibes. The farmer's markets in Phoenix offer a unique shopping experience that celebrates local growers, artisans, and food producers.

One famous farmer's market is the Downtown Phoenix Farmers Market in downtown Phoenix. In addition to the delicious produce, visitors can find local crafts, handmade goods, and food trucks serving tasty treats. The Uptown Farmers Market is another must-visit destination known for its live music and vibrant atmosphere; it's a great place to spend a Saturday morning and connect with the local community.

For those seeking an authentic experience, the Singh Meadows Farmers Market focuses on sustainable and organic practices, offering an assortment of fresh produce, artisanal products, and gourmet foods.

The farmer's markets in Phoenix offer an opportunity to shop for fresh and locally sourced goods and serve as community gathering places. Visitors can meet the growers and artisans, learn about sustainable practices, and support the local economy. Some Farmer's Markets shut down for the summer due to extreme heat, even in the early mornings. Please check the websites to ensure your favorite destination is open during your visit.

Downtown Phoenix Farmers Market

The Downtown Phoenix Farmers Market is popular with food lovers and community enthusiasts. Located in the heart of downtown Phoenix, visitors can explore a variety of vendors offering locally grown fruits, vegetables, meats, and dairy products, as well as unique offerings like handmade crafts, baked goods, and food trucks. The market features live music, cooking demonstrations, and a lively atmosphere that fosters a sense of community.

720 N 5th St, Phoenix, AZ 85004
(602) 625-6736
Saturday 7am-10:30am
www.downtownphoenixfarmersmarket.org

Uptown Farmers Market

This Market is a bustling hub of fresh and local produce, artisanal goods, and community spirit. This vibrant market is known for its diverse selection of organic fruits, vegetables, herbs, and specialty products from local farmers and vendors. Visitors can browse a range of homemade baked goods, unique crafts, and gourmet treats. The market also hosts live music performances, educational workshops, and interactive activities, creating an engaging atmosphere. With its emphasis on supporting local growers and artisans, the Uptown Farmers Market offers a delightful experience that connects people with fresh, sustainable, and locally sourced products while fostering a sense of community.

5757 N Central Ave, Phoenix, AZ 85012
(602) 859-5648
Saturdays 7am-11pm
www.uptownmarketaz.com

Tempe Farmer's Market

This indoor farmer's market is open daily, allows you to shop for groceries from local growers, and provides a deli, coffee shop, and bakery. The Tempe Farmer's Market specializes in Vegetarian, Vegan, and Gluten Free options for those with specific diets. This is a must-stop shop, especially if you accidentally slept in on the weekends!

805 S Farmer Ave, Tempe, AZ 85281
(480) 557-9970
Monday-Sunday 11am-8pm
www.tempefarmersmarket.com

Singh Meadows Farmer's Market

Also, in Tempe, a family-owned farm offers a unique and serene shopping experience surrounded by lush greenery. This market emphasizes sustainability and organic practices and uniquely offers compost for your home garden. Visitors can browse through a curated selection of fruits, vegetables, artisanal goods, and specialty items while enjoying the tranquil atmosphere of the meadow. The market also hosts educational workshops, live music performances, and community events, providing a space for people to connect with local growers, artisans, and like-minded individuals. The Singh Meadows Farmers Market is a hidden gem that offers a peaceful and eco-conscious shopping experience for those seeking high-quality, sustainably sourced products.

1490 E Weber Dr, Tempe, AZ 85281
(480) 225-7199
Hours are sporadic; check the Facebook page for details to plan your visit.
www.facebook.com/SinghMeadows

Park West Market

This huge Market on the West Side of Phoenix offers more than just Farmer's goods. You'll find homemade home goods such as soaps, candles, and accessories. Enjoy homemade bread, jerky, salsas, and even dog treats! There's something for everyone at the Park West Market. This location also hosts special events like a Christmas Market and a Mother's Day Out that bring in extra vendors that offer specialized products related to the theme.

9744 W. Norther Ave. Peoria, AZ 85345
(602) 884-9882
October-April Saturdays 9am-1pm
May-September Every 3rd Saturday 8am-12pm
www.theparkwestmarket.com

Shopping Centers

ACTIVITIES

Biltmore Fashion Square

The Biltmore Fashion Square is a prestigious shopping center in Phoenix, Arizona, known for its upscale and luxurious offerings. Its sophisticated ambiance and stylish architecture provide a premier shopping experience. The mall boasts a curated selection of high-end brands, designer stores, and exclusive boutiques, attracting fashion enthusiasts and trendsetters. Additionally, Biltmore Fashion Square features a variety of fine dining options, making it a perfect destination for a day of indulgence and sophistication.

  2502 E Camelback Rd, Phoenix, AZ 85016
  (602) 955-8400
  www.shopbiltmore.com

Scottsdale Quarter

This open-air shopping center in Scottsdale has a modern and upscale atmosphere that offers a unique shopping experience. The Quarter features an impressive collection of high-end fashion brands, luxury retailers, specialty stores, and live entertainment. The Quarter also hosts a diverse range of dining from casual eateries to fine restaurants, making it a perfect destination to shop 'til you drop.

  15279 N Scottsdale Rd Ste 260, Scottsdale, AZ 85254
  (480) 270-8123
  www.scottsdalequarter.com

The Shops at Gainey Village

The Shops at Gainey Village is known for its charming Mediterranean-style architecture and beautiful courtyard setting. It offers a delightful shopping experience showcasing a diverse range of boutique shops, specialty stores, and designer brands. It offers a mix of fashion, accessories, home decor, and unique gifts. Visitors can indulge in dining options ranging from casual cafes to upscale restaurants and enjoy live music and events.

8777 N Scottsdale Rd, Scottsdale, AZ 85253

(480) 398-2222

www.theshopsgaineyvillage.com

Westgate Entertainment District

This bustling entertainment complex is located in Glendale and offers a diverse mix of shopping, dining, and entertainment options for visitors of all ages. The district features a wide range of popular retailers, restaurants, and specialty stores, allowing shoppers to explore a variety of fashion, accessories, and unique products. In addition, Westgate is home to a vibrant nightlife with numerous bars, clubs, and live music venues. Visitors can also catch sporting events at the adjacent State Farm Stadium or enjoy family-friendly activities like pickleball, mini golf, and escape rooms.

6770 N Sunrise Blvd, Glendale, AZ 85305

(480) 387-5678

www.westgateaz.com

The Melrose District

This vibrant and eclectic neighborhood is known for its vintage shops, retro boutiques, and unique charm. It offers a treasure trove of one-of-a-kind finds, including vintage clothing, furniture, artwork, and collectibles. The Melrose District also hosts regular street fairs and events, attracting art enthusiasts, fashion lovers, and vintage aficionados. You'll also find delicious restaurants and LGBTQ+ nightclubs, making the Melrose District a one-stop shop morning, noon, and night.

7th Avenue between Indian School Rd. and Camelback

www.visitphoenix.com/lgbtq/melrose-district

Arizona Mills Mall

This trendy shopping destination is located in Tempe and is one of the largest indoor outlet malls in the state. It offers an extensive selection of stores, making it a shopper's paradise, with over 185 retailers, including fashion, accessories, home goods, electronics, and more. The mall also features entertainment options like a cinema, restaurants, and family-friendly attractions like a carousel and mini-golf.

5000 S Arizona Mills Cir, Tempe, AZ 85282

(480) 491-9700

www.simon.com/mall/arizona-mills

SPAS

Phoenix, Arizona, is home to a plethora of world-class spas that offer luxurious and rejuvenating experiences. From relaxing massages to invigorating facials, these spas provide a sanctuary of tranquility and pampering.

One renowned spa in Phoenix is the Joya Spa at Omni Scottsdale Resort & Spa at Montelucia. This Moroccan-inspired oasis features lavish treatment rooms, a Hammam, and a rooftop pool, allowing guests to unwind in a serene atmosphere.

For a unique spa experience, the Alvadora Spa at Royal Palms Resort and Spa combines Mediterranean-inspired treatments with lush gardens and tranquil courtyards, providing a serene escape from the city.

Phoenix also offers wellness-focused spas, such as the Phoenician Spa, which offers a range of holistic therapies, fitness classes, and wellness consultations.

Whether you're seeking relaxation, beauty treatments, or wellness experiences, the spas in Phoenix provide a haven of indulgence and self-care. With their skilled therapists, serene environments, and luxurious amenities, these spas offer an escape from the every day and an opportunity to rejuvenate the mind, body, and spirit.

Joya Spa

Located in the Omni Scottsdale Resort & Spa at Montelucia, the Joya Spa is a luxurious and tranquil retreat. Inspired by the enchanting essence of Morocco, this world-class spa offers a wide range of indulgent treatments and experiences. Guests can relax in the Hammam, enjoy rejuvenating massages, facials, and body treatments, or unwind in the rooftop pool with breathtaking views of the surrounding desert landscape. With its serene ambiance, skilled therapists, and opulent facilities, Joya Spa provides a haven of relaxation and rejuvenation, inviting guests to escape the stresses of daily life and embark on a well-being journey.

4949 E Lincoln Dr, Paradise Valley, AZ 85253
(480) 627-3020
Hours: Monday-Sunday 8:30am-7pm
www.omnihotels.com/hotels/scottsdale-montelucia/wellness

Alvadora Spa

Tucked in Royal Palms Resort and Spa, you'll find a serene oasis combining Mediterranean-inspired luxury and peaceful surroundings. Nestled amidst lush gardens and tranquil courtyards, the spa offers rejuvenating treatments that draw upon ancient wellness traditions. Guests can indulge in massages, facials, body wraps, and other indulgent therapies that nourish the body and relax the mind. With its serene ambiance, skilled therapists, and attention to detail, the Alvadora Spa provides a sanctuary of relaxation and tranquility.

5200 E Camelback Rd, Phoenix, AZ 85018
(602) 977-6400
Hours: Monday-Sunday 8:30am-5pm
www.hyatt.com/en-US/spas/Alvadora-Spa/home

Phoenician Spa

Nestled in the luxurious Phoenician Resort, this world-class spa offers a wide array of holistic treatments, rejuvenating therapies, and wellness services. Guests can indulge in therapeutic massages, facials, body wraps, and beauty treatments, all designed to promote relaxation, rejuvenation, and balance. With its serene atmosphere, skilled therapists, and state-of-the-art facilities, the Phoenician Spa provides a holistic approach to wellness, offering guests an opportunity to restore and revitalize their mind, body, and spirit. Whether seeking relaxation, healing, or a comprehensive wellness experience, the Phoenician Spa is a sanctuary where guests can unwind and reconnect with themselves. The website recommends reservations be made at least 3-4 weeks before your stay to ensure availability.

  6000 E Camelback Rd, Scottsdale, AZ 85251

  (480) 423-2452

  Hours: Monday-Sunday 9:30am-5:30pm

  www.thephoenician.com/spa

Hawaiian Experience Spa

Located in Goodyear, this family-owned spa is one of the few on the valley's west side. This unique spa offers a range of Hawaiian-inspired treatments that transport guests to a tropical paradise. From traditional Lomi Lomi massages to invigorating body scrubs and luxurious facials, each treatment is designed to create a profoundly relaxing and rejuvenating experience. The spa's serene ambiance, soothing music, and skilled therapists provide a tranquil escape from the outside world.

  13778 W McDowell Rd # 304, Goodyear, AZ 85395

  (623) 536-7766

  Hours: Monday-Sunday 9am-9pm

  www.hawaiianexperiencespa.com

The Spa at the Victory Club

For those looking for luxury in the West Valley, The Spa at the Victory Club in Buckeye is a hidden gem in a luxury residential community. This serene and exclusive spa offers a range of indulgent treatments, including massages, facials, body wraps, and more. Guests can immerse themselves in the tranquil ambiance and enjoy personalized services tailored to their needs. The spa features state-of-the-art facilities, including relaxation lounges, steam rooms, and outdoor treatment areas, providing a luxurious and rejuvenating experience. With its attentive staff, serene surroundings, and wellness offerings, The Spa at the Victory Club is a haven of relaxation and an ideal destination for self-care and rejuvenation.

5325 N Verrado Way, Buckeye, AZ 85396

(623) 533-5422

Hours: Monday-Saturday 9am-5pm; Sunday 9am-4pm

www.spaatvictoryclub.com

FITNESS

The fitness scene in Phoenix, Arizona, is vibrant and diverse, offering a range of options to cater to various interests and fitness levels. The city has numerous gyms, fitness studios, and outdoor activities catering to locals and visitors.

Gym enthusiasts can find many well-equipped fitness centers offering state-of-the-art equipment, group classes, and personal training services. Popular gym chains like LA Fitness, 24-Hour Fitness, and Anytime Fitness have multiple locations throughout the city.

For those who prefer a more specialized approach, Phoenix offers a variety of boutique fitness studios. From yoga and Pilates to CrossFit and cycling, there are studios that cater to almost every fitness discipline. Some notable studios include The Madison, BODI, and The Phoenix Effect.

Phoenix's sunny climate also lends itself well to outdoor activities. Hiking enthusiasts can explore the city's scenic trails, such as Camelback Mountain and Piestewa Peak. The city's extensive trail systems, parks, and outdoor spaces provide opportunities for jogging, biking, and outdoor fitness classes.

Additionally, Phoenix hosts various fitness events and races throughout the year, including marathons, triathlons, and fun runs, offering opportunities for both competitive and recreational athletes to participate.

With its wide range of fitness options, whether it's hitting the gym, practicing yoga, or enjoying outdoor activities, Phoenix provides a thriving fitness scene promoting a healthy and active lifestyle for residents and visitors alike.

Urban Yoga Phoenix

This popular yoga studio is located in downtown Phoenix. Known for its welcoming atmosphere and experienced instructors, it provides yoga classes for practitioners of all levels. From gentle flow and restorative sessions to dynamic vinyasa and power yoga, Urban Yoga provides diverse practices to suit individual preferences. The studio's modern and spacious setting creates a tranquil environment for relaxation, mindfulness, and physical well-being. With its focus on community and holistic wellness, Urban Yoga Phoenix has become a go-to destination for yoga enthusiasts seeking a peaceful and rejuvenating experience in the heart of the city.

2024 N 7th St #201, Phoenix, AZ 85006

(602) 277-9642

www.urbanyogaphx.com

Remedy Pilates and Barre

This premier fitness studio has locations in Scottsdale and Arcadia. With its dedicated team of certified instructors and state-of-the-art equipment, Remedy offers a range of classes that focus on strength, flexibility, and overall body conditioning. Whether it's a Pilates reformer class or a dynamic barre session, clients can expect a challenging and effective workout that targets specific muscle groups. The studio's welcoming and supportive environment caters to individuals of all fitness levels, making it a popular choice for those seeking a low-impact yet highly effective workout that promotes physical fitness and overall well-being.

6949 E Shea Blvd #115 Scottsdale, AZ 85254

(480) 699-8160

3629 E Indian School Road Phoenix, Arizona 85018

(602) 237-6489

https://www.remedypilates.com/

Frame

This new HIIT training facility focuses on small classes or one-to-one fitness. They specialize in connecting the mind, body, and spirit to maximize your results in a positive, energizing atmosphere. They offer a free introductory class, so stop by on your visit and see if a small package of classes is right for you.

1806 N. Scottsdale Rd., Tempe, AZ 85281

www.frametempe.com

The MMA Lab

This mixed martial arts training facility has produced top-level fighters in various disciplines. Led by skilled coaches and trainers, the lab offers comprehensive training programs for individuals of all skill levels, from beginners to professional fighters. The facility is equipped with state-of-the-art training equipment, and it provides a supportive and disciplined environment for athletes to improve their skills in disciplines such as Brazilian Jiu-Jitsu, Muay Thai, wrestling, and boxing. With its commitment to excellence and a focus on physical and mental conditioning, the MMA Lab has established itself as a premier destination for those passionate about mixed martial arts in Phoenix.

2710 W Bell Rd #1150, Phoenix, AZ 85053

(623) 792-8543

www.mmalab.com

Rumble Boxing

Rumble Boxing combines high-intensity boxing training with music and entertainment. With locations in Tempe and Gilbert, Rumble Boxing offers dynamic group classes led by experienced trainers who guide participants through a full-body workout incorporating boxing techniques and cardio exercises. The energetic and immersive atmosphere and pulsating music create an engaging and motivating environment. Rumble Boxing is suitable for all fitness levels, providing a fun and challenging workout that enhances strength, endurance, and overall fitness. It has gained popularity for its unique blend of boxing-inspired training, energetic ambiance, and community spirit

   430 N Scottsdale Rd Suite A-115, Tempe, AZ 85281
   (602) 675-0530
   325 N Ash St, Gilbert, AZ 85233
   (480) 597-4184
   www.rumbleboxinggym.com

Sweatshop on Central

This fitness studio offers a variety of classes, including yoga, barre, and spin. With a focus on holistic wellness, the studio provides a welcoming and inclusive environment for participants of all fitness levels. Whether it's a dynamic spin class, a calming yoga session, or a challenging barre workout, Sweatshop on Central aims to empower individuals and help them achieve their health and fitness goals. The experienced instructors and supportive community foster a positive and motivating atmosphere, making Sweatshop on Central a perfect destination for those seeking a well-rounded fitness experience in Phoenix.

   100 E Camelback Rd #156, Phoenix, AZ 85012
   (602) 603-1891
   www.sweatshopcentral.com

5

Sports and Gaming

Phoenix, Arizona, offers a dynamic blend of sports and gambling experiences for enthusiasts seeking excitement and entertainment. The city is home to professional sports teams and Native American casinos.

Sports fans can immerse themselves in the electric atmosphere of live sporting events. Phoenix boasts teams in major sports leagues, including the Phoenix Suns (NBA), Arizona Cardinals (NFL), Arizona Diamondbacks (MLB), and Arizona Coyotes (NHL). These teams compete in state-of-the-art arenas and stadiums, hosting thrilling games annually.

For those seeking a different kind of excitement, Phoenix is surrounded by Native American casinos that offer live entertainment, luxury restaurants, and thrilling gaming tables. Casinos like Talking Stick Resort, Casino Arizona, and Wild Horse Pass Hotel & Casino feature exciting slot machines, table games, poker rooms, and live entertainment options. Visitors can try their luck at blackjack, roulette, or poker while enjoying the vibrant atmosphere and live performances.

Whether it's the thrill of live sports, the excitement of casino gaming, or a combination of both, Phoenix provides a diverse range of experiences for sports and gambling enthusiasts.

NATIONAL BASKETBALL ASSOCIATION (NBA)

The Phoenix Suns

The Phoenix Suns are a professional basketball team in Downtown Phoenix and are an integral part of the city's sports culture. The team competes in the National Basketball Association (NBA) and has a rich history of success, including multiple playoff appearances and a trip to the NBA Finals in 2021. The Suns call the Footprint Center home, formerly known as the Talking Stick Resort Arena.

The Footprint Center is a state-of-the-art sports and entertainment venue in downtown Phoenix. With a seating capacity of over 18,000, it provides a thrilling atmosphere for fans to cheer on their beloved Suns. The arena features modern amenities, high-definition video screens, and excellent acoustics, ensuring an immersive experience for spectators.

Beyond basketball, the Footprint Center hosts various concerts, shows, and other sporting events throughout the year. It has been a venue for significant events, including the NBA All-Star Game in 1995 and the WNBA Finals. The facility's central location allows easy access to downtown amenities, restaurants, and nightlife, making it a vibrant entertainment hub.

The Phoenix Suns and the Footprint Center have become a source of pride for the city, uniting fans and creating memorable experiences.

The Footprint Center
201 E Jefferson St, Phoenix, AZ 85004
(602) 379-7800
www.footprintcenter.com

NATIONAL FOOTBALL LEAGUE (NFL)

The Arizona Cardinals

The Arizona Cardinals are a professional football team in Glendale and were featured in the HBO Docuseries "Hard Knocks in Season: The Arizona Cardinals" in 2022. The team competes in the National Football League

(NFL) and has a dedicated fan base that fills the stadium with energy and excitement on game days. The Cardinals play their home games at State Farm Stadium, a modern and impressive venue widely regarded as one of the premier stadiums in the NFL.

State Farm Stadium offers a seating capacity of over 63,000 and is known for its retractable roof and field. This innovative feature allows the stadium to host various events throughout the year, and it was honored to host Super Bowl LVII in 2023. With its state-of-the-art facilities, comfortable seating, and excellent sightlines, State Farm Stadium provides fans with an immersive and unforgettable experience.

Beyond football, the stadium has hosted numerous high-profile events, including college football bowl games and international soccer matches. It has become a focal point for major sporting and entertainment events in the region, drawing visitors from near and far.

State Farm Stadium's convenient location in the Westgate Entertainment District allows fans to enjoy a range of amenities before and after games. The district features restaurants, bars, shops, and entertainment options, creating a lively and vibrant atmosphere.

The Arizona Cardinals and State Farm Stadium have become synonymous with the city of Phoenix, bringing people together and providing thrilling sports experiences. The team's performance and the state-of-the-art stadium contribute to the pride and enthusiasm surrounding the Cardinals and their loyal fan base.

State Farm Stadium
1 Cardinals Dr, Glendale, AZ 85305
(623) 433-7101
www.statefarmstadium.com

MAJOR LEAGUE BASEBALL (MLB)

The Arizona Diamondbacks

The Arizona Diamondbacks are a professional baseball team also in Downtown Phoenix. As a Major League Baseball (MLB) member, This National League Team has brought excitement and success to the city since its inception in 1998. The team's home games are played at Chase Field, a modern and fan-friendly stadium located in downtown Phoenix.

Chase Field offers a seating capacity of over 48,000 and is known for its unique retractable roof, which allows games to be played comfortably in any weather condition. The stadium's design provides excellent sightlines and an intimate viewing experience for fans, ensuring that every seat offers a great view of the action on the field.

Beyond baseball, Chase Field has hosted a variety of events, including concerts, college football games, and international soccer matches. The venue's versatility and state-of-the-art facilities make it a popular destination for sports and entertainment.

The Diamondbacks' success on the field, including winning the World Series in 2001, has fostered a passionate fan base that fills the stadium with energy and support. The team's commitment to community engagement and creating a memorable fan experience has further endeared them to the city.

Located in the heart of downtown Phoenix, Chase Field is surrounded by a vibrant mix of restaurants, bars, and entertainment options. This provides fans with a plethora of pre-and post-game activities, enhancing the overall experience of attending a Diamondbacks game.

Chase Field
401 E Jefferson St, Phoenix, AZ 85004
(602) 514-8400
www.dbacks.com

MLB Spring Training

A unique attraction in Phoenix is Spring Training for The Cactus League.

During spring training, fans can watch their favorite teams up close and personal in a more relaxed and intimate atmosphere. The weather is typically ideal, making it a perfect outing for families, friends, and baseball enthusiasts.

The Cactus League games provide an opportunity for players to fine-tune their skills and for teams to evaluate new talent. It is a critical period before the regular season begins, and the excitement and anticipation in the air are palpable. There are around 200 games played in the greater Phoenix Metro area from late February to late March, so there's a game to fit any schedule. But be sure to come prepared. Popular teams' tickets can sell out fast, and since the stadiums are more low-key, there's less shade, so protect yourself with sunscreen and a hat!

Overall, spring training in Phoenix is a baseball lover's paradise. The combination of top-notch facilities, beautiful weather, and the chance to witness the preseason action of multiple teams creates an unforgettable experience for fans. It's an annual tradition that brings joy and excitement to the city and sets the stage for the upcoming MLB season.

Salt River Fields at Talking Stick
Spring Home of the Arizona Diamondbacks & Colorado Rockies
7555 N Pima Rd, Scottsdale, AZ 85258
(480) 270-5000
www.saltriverfields.com

Sloan Park
Spring Home of the Chicago Cubs
2330 W Rio Salado Pkwy, Mesa, AZ 85201
(480) 668-0500
www.mlb.com/cubs/sloan-park

Camelback Ranch
Spring Home of the Chicago White Sox & Los Angeles Dodgers
10710 W Camelback Rd, Phoenix, AZ 85037
(623) 302-5000
www.mlb.com/camelback-ranch

Goodyear Ballpark
Spring Home of the Cincinnati Reds & Cleveland Guardians
1933 S Ballpark Way, Goodyear, AZ 85338
(623) 882-3120
www.goodyearbp.com

Surprise Stadium
Spring Home of the Kansas City Royals & Texas Rangers
15850 N Bullard Ave, Surprise, AZ 85374
(623) 222-2222
www.surprisestadium.com

Tempe Diablo Stadium
Spring Home of the Los Angeles Angels
2200 W Alameda Dr, Tempe, AZ 85282
(480) 350-5205
www.tempe.gov/government/community-services/community-recreation-centers/diablo-stadium

American Family Fields of Phoenix
Spring Home of the Milwaukee Brewers
3805 N 53rd Ave, Phoenix, AZ 85031
(623) 245-5500
www.mlb.com/brewers/spring-training/ballpark

Hohokam Stadium
Spring Home of the Oakland A's
1235 N Center St, Mesa, AZ 85201
(480) 644-4451
www.mlb.com/athletics/spring-training/ballpark

Peoria Sports Complex
Spring Home of the San Diego Padres & Seattle Mariners

16101 N 83rd Ave, Peoria, AZ 85382
(623) 773-8700
www.peoriasportscomplex.com

Scottsdale Stadium
Spring Home of the San Francisco Giants
7408 E Osborn Rd, Scottsdale, AZ 85251
(480) 312-2586
www.scottsdaleaz.gov/scottsdale-stadium

NATIONAL HOCKEY LEAGUE (NHL)

The Arizona Coyotes

The Arizona Coyotes are a professional ice hockey team currently in Tempe. They are a member of the National Hockey League (NHL) and are an integral part of the sports culture in the Phoenix metropolitan area. Since their relocation from Winnipeg in 1996, the Coyotes have captured the hearts of hockey fans in Arizona. The team has had its ups and downs but has remained committed to building a solid franchise.

The Coyotes' home games used to be played at Gila River Arena in Glendale but did not renew their lease when plans for a new Tempe Arena were drawn. Unfortunately, the voters denied the bid, and the Coyotes were forced to sign a three-year lease at Mullett Arena. The team's dedicated fan base, known as the "Yotes Nation," fills the arena with energy and passion, creating an electric environment on game nights.

Over the years, the Coyotes have had notable successes, including several playoff appearances and a trip to the Western Conference Finals. The team has showcased talented players, developed prospects, and built a competitive roster that continues to evolve.

Off the ice, the Coyotes have established themselves as active community participants, engaging in various charitable initiatives and supporting local causes.

Since the Arizona Coyotes are currently in a temporary home, I'll direct you to their website for details about how to catch a hockey game.

www.nhl.com/coyotes

GOLF

Waste Management Phoenix Open (PGA)

This is one of the most unique and highly anticipated events on the PGA Tour, known for its energetic atmosphere and record-breaking attendance.

The tournament takes place at TPC Scottsdale's Stadium Course, which is transformed into a lively and boisterous venue for the event. The famous par-3 16th hole, known as "The Coliseum," is the epicenter of the tournament's electrifying energy. Spectators line the stadium-like stands surrounding the hole, creating a raucous atmosphere reminiscent of a sporting event rather than a golf tournament.

The Waste Management Phoenix Open stands out for its commitment to sustainability and environmental initiatives. Waste Management, the title sponsor, emphasizes recycling and waste reduction throughout the event, showcasing their dedication to environmental responsibility.

Beyond the golf, the tournament features an array of entertainment options. The Birds Nest, a popular concert venue, hosts top musical acts each night, adding to the festival-like atmosphere surrounding the event.

The Waste Management Phoenix Open has gained a reputation for being the most well-attended golf tournament on the PGA Tour. Its unique blend of professional golf, enthusiastic fans, and a festive atmosphere make it an unparalleled experience for players and spectators.

Notably, the tournament has also made significant charitable contributions over the years. The Waste Management Phoenix Open is consistently recognized as one of the most charitable events on the PGA Tour, with proceeds benefiting local nonprofits and organizations.

The Waste Management Phoenix Open is much more than a golf tournament. It's a one-of-a-kind event that combines world-class golf, enthusiastic fans, sustainability initiatives, and entertainment, making it a must-see experience for golf and sports enthusiasts alike.

TPC Scottsdale

17020 N Hayden Rd, Scottsdale, AZ 85255

(480) 585-4334

https://tpc.com/scottsdale/waste-management-phoenix-open/

Top 5 Golf Courses in Phoenix

Phoenix, Arizona, is a golfer's paradise, offering a wide array of golf courses and a year-round favorable climate. With over 200 golf courses in the Greater Phoenix area, players of all skill levels can find their perfect course.

Phoenix boasts championship courses designed by renowned architects, including Jack Nicklaus, Tom Fazio, and Robert Trent Jones Jr. The diversity of courses caters to various playing styles and preferences, from desert-style layouts to lush green fairways with stunning mountain backdrops.

The city's favorable climate allows for year-round golfing, with mild winters and warm, dry summers. This means golfers can enjoy their favorite sport regardless of the season.

The city also offers excellent golf amenities, including golf resorts, professional instruction, and practice facilities. Many courses provide top-notch clubhouse amenities, dining options, and stunning views.

Desert Mountain Golf Club

37700 N Desert Mountain Pkwy, Scottsdale, AZ 85262

(480) 595-4000

www.desertmountain.com/golf

Mirabel Golf Club

37100 N Mirabel Club Dr, Scottsdale, AZ 85262

(480) 437-1500

www.mirabel.com

Wigwam Golf Club

451 N Old Litchfield Rd, Litchfield Park, AZ 85340

(623) 935-9414

www.wigwamgolf.com

Troon North Golf Club

10320 E Dynamite Blvd, Scottsdale, AZ 85262

(480) 585-5300

www.troonnorthgolf.com

Ak-Chin Southern Dunes Golf Club

48456 AZ-238, Maricopa, AZ 85139

(480) 367-8949

www.akchinsoutherndunes.com

CASINOS

Phoenix, Arizona, is home to a vibrant casino scene that offers a variety of gaming and entertainment options. Native American tribes operate most of the casinos in the area, providing visitors with a unique and culturally rich experience.

Casinos like Talking Stick Resort, Casino Arizona, and Wild Horse Pass Hotel & Casino offer various gaming opportunities. These establishments feature slot machines, table games like blackjack, poker rooms, and bingo halls. Whether you're a novice or an experienced gambler, there's something for everyone.

Beyond the gaming floors, the casinos in Phoenix also provide visitors with a host of amenities. Many offer luxurious hotel accommodations, fine dining options, live entertainment venues, and spas for relaxation and rejuvenation.

In addition to the gaming and amenities, the casinos often host concerts, comedy shows, and other live performances, attracting top-notch entertainment acts and creating a lively atmosphere for visitors.

It's important to note that the legal gambling age in Arizona is 21 years old, and proper identification is required to enter the casinos.

What sets the casinos in Phoenix apart is their Native American heritage. These establishments offer an opportunity to experience the rich culture and traditions of the Native American tribes that operate them. Visitors can learn about tribal history, art, and crafts while enjoying the excitement of the gaming experience.

Talking Stick Resort

9800 Talking Stick Way, Scottsdale, AZ 85256

(480) 850-7777

www.talkingstickresort.com

Casino Arizona

524 N 92nd St, Scottsdale, AZ 85256

(480) 850-7777

www.casinoarizona.com

Gila River Resorts & Casinos - Wild Horse Pass

5040 Wild Horse Pass Blvd, Chandler, AZ 85226

(800) 946-4452

www.playatgila.com

Harrah's Ak-Chin Casino

15406 N Maricopa Rd, Maricopa, AZ 85139

(480) 802-5000

www.caesars.com/harrahs-ak-chin

Gila River Resorts & Casinos - Vee Quiva

15091 S Komatke Ln, Laveen Village, AZ 85339

(800) 946-4452

www.playatgila.com

ARIZONA STATE UNIVERSITY

Arizona State University (ASU) boasts a rich athletic tradition, with its Sun Devils teams competing at the NCAA Division I level as part of the Pac-12 Conference. ASU's athletics program is known for its competitiveness, success, and passionate fan base.

The Sun Devils compete in a wide range of sports, including football, basketball, baseball, softball, soccer, volleyball, and more. The football team, in particular, has a storied history and plays its home games at Sun Devil Stadium, creating an electric atmosphere on game days.

ASU's state-of-the-art athletic facilities provide student-athletes with excellent training and competition venues. These include the Sun Devil Stadium, Wells Fargo Arena, Phoenix Municipal Stadium, and the Mona Plummer Aquatic Center.

Beyond the on-field success, ASU strongly emphasizes the academic success and overall well-being of its student-athletes. The university provides comprehensive support services, including academic advising, tutoring, and access to top-notch training facilities.

ASU's athletic program also emphasizes community engagement and outreach. The Sun Devils participate in various philanthropic activities, promoting positive change and giving back to the community.

The Sun Devils have achieved numerous accolades and championships over the years, with several individual athletes representing ASU at the highest levels of their respective sports.

Attending an ASU athletic event is a thrilling experience, with enthusiastic fans filling the stands and supporting their teams. The university's commitment to excellence and strong athletic tradition make ASU a powerhouse in college sports.

Overall, athletics at Arizona State University provides a platform for student-athletes to excel on and off the field. ASU's Sun Devils teams showcase talent, passion, and a commitment to success, contributing to the vibrant sports culture in Phoenix and representing the university with pride.

TRAVEL TO PHOENIX, ARIZONA

500 East Veterans Way Tempe, AZ 85287
(480) 727-0000
www.thesundevils.com

6

Restaurants, Bars, & Bakeries

CASUAL DINING

Danky's Bar-B-Q - $$

A hidden gem for barbecue enthusiasts. This family-owned and operated establishment offers a mouthwatering selection of smoked meats, including brisket, pulled pork, ribs, and chicken, all prepared with a perfect blend of spices and love. The menu also features delicious sides like macaroni and cheese, coleslaw, and baked beans. With a warm and welcoming atmosphere, Danky's BBQ creates a memorable dining experience for its customers. Whether you dine in or opt for takeout, visiting Danky's BBQ promises a finger-licking and satisfying barbecue feast that keeps patrons coming back for more.

4727 E Bell Rd #31, Phoenix, AZ 85032
(602) 996-2016
Hours: Monday-Saturday 11am-8pm; Sunday 11am-6pm
www.dankysbbq.com

The Stand Arcadia Burger Shoppe - $

A burger lover's delight. This cozy and retro-style eatery serves up delicious, handcrafted burgers made from fresh, high-quality ingredients. With a diverse menu that includes classic favorites and creative specialty burgers, there's something to satisfy every craving. The Stand is proud to use locally sourced produce and support the community. They offer tasty sides like sweet potato fries and onion rings alongside their mouthwatering burgers.

3538 E Indian School Rd, Phoenix, AZ 85018

(602) 314-5259

Hours: Monday-Tuesday Closed; Wednesday-Sunday 11am-9pm

www.thestandphx.com

Matt's Big Breakfast - $$

A beloved breakfast spot with three locations in Phoenix known for its delicious, hearty meals. This small, unassuming diner has earned a big reputation for its made-from-scratch dishes and use of fresh, locally sourced ingredients. The menu features a variety of seemingly classic breakfast favorites, including fluffy pancakes, crispy bacon, and perfectly cooked eggs, but Matt has inspired twists. Whether you opt for their famous "Chop and Chick" pork chop and eggs or their mouthwatering omelets, the quality and taste are unmatched. With a warm and inviting atmosphere, Matt's Big Breakfast has become a must-visit destination for locals and tourists seeking a satisfying breakfast experience.

825 N 1st St, Phoenix, AZ 85004

(602) 254-1074

7507 W Rose Garden Ln #107, Glendale, AZ 85308

(623) 259-9836

3118 E Camelback Rd, Phoenix, AZ 85016

(602) 840-3450

Hours: Monday-Sunday 7am-2 pm

www.mattsbigbreakfast.com

The Vig - $$

With 6 locations around the Phoenix Metro, The Vig is a trendy and vibrant restaurant and bar offering a chic yet relaxed atmosphere for patrons to enjoy. With multiple locations throughout the city, The Vig is known for its stylish outdoor patios, inviting indoor spaces, and a menu catering to diverse tastes. Whether it's brunch, lunch, or dinner, The Vig serves up an array of delectable dishes, craft cocktails, and a selection of local beers. The combination of great food, drinks, and an energetic ambiance makes The Vig popular for socializing and unwinding with friends and family.

Fillmore

606 N 4th Ave, Phoenix, AZ 85003

(602) 254-2242

Hours: Monday-Thursday 11am-10 pm; Friday 11 am-11 pm; Saturday 10 am-11 pm; Sunday 10am-10 pm

Park West

9824 W Northern Ave #1840, Peoria, AZ 85345

(623) 231-7597

Hours: Monday-Thursday 11 am-10 pm; Friday 11 am-11 pm; Saturday 10 am-11 pm; Sunday 10 am-10 pm

Arcadia

4041 N 40th St, Phoenix, AZ 85018

(602) 553-7227

Hours: Monday-Thursday 11 am-10 pm; Friday 11 am-11 pm; Saturday 10 am-11 pm; Sunday 10 am-10 pm

North Central

8729 N Central Ave, Phoenix, AZ 85020

(602) 606-2258

Hours: Monday-Thursday 3 pm-9 pm; Friday 3 pm-10 pm; Saturday 10 am-10 pm; Sunday 10 am-9pm

McCormick Ranch

7345 N Vía Paseo Del Sur, Scottsdale, AZ 85258

(480) 758-5399

Hours: Monday-Thursday 11 am-10 pm; Friday 11 am-11 pm; Saturday 10 am-11 pm; Sunday 10 am-10 pm

McDowell Mountain

10199 E Bell Rd, Scottsdale, AZ 85260

(480) 935-2949

Hours: Monday-Thursday 11 am-10 pm; Friday 11 am-11 pm; Saturday 10 am-11 pm; Sunday 10 am-10 pm

www.thevig.us

Cuff - $$

Cuff is one of the newest restaurants in this section, a laid-back, casual New American restaurant and bar. This locally owned gem seamlessly fuses classic American faves with cultural twists from around the world. The menu boasts an enticing mix of traditional and innovative cocktails, complemented by boutique wines and cold craft beer. Various dietary preferences, including vegan, vegetarian, and gluten-free options, are peppered throughout the menu, so Cuff provides something for everyone. Murphey Park is becoming the perfect spot for a quick business lunch, a leisurely dinner, or happy hour.

7021 N 58th Ave, Glendale, AZ 85301

(623) 847-8890

Hours: Sunday-Monday Closed; Tuesday-Saturday 11 am-9 pm

www.cuffglendale.com

CULTURAL MENUS

Pomo Pizzeria - $$

Pomo is a celebrated Italian restaurant that brings the authentic taste of Naples to Phoenix. With a dedication to using high-quality ingredients and traditional wood-fired ovens, Pomo Pizzeria serves up mouthwatering Neapolitan-style pizzas that are both rustic and refined. The menu extends beyond pizzas to include a variety of delectable antipasti, pasta, and salads, all inspired by classic Italian flavors. The inviting ambiance, attentive service, and extensive wine selection create a delightful dining experience. Pomo Pizzeria captures the essence of Italian cuisine, making it a must-visit destination for pizza lovers and Italian food enthusiasts in the Phoenix area.

705 N 1st St UNIT 120, Phoenix, AZ 85004

(602) 795-2555

2502 E Camelback Rd STE A&B, Phoenix, AZ 85016

(602) 954-5221

8977 N Scottsdale Rd #504, Scottsdale, AZ 85253

(480) 998-1366

Hours: Sunday-Thursday 11 am-9 pm; Friday-Saturday 11 am-10 pm

www.pomopizzeria.com

Gallo Blanco - $$

A vibrant Mexican restaurant offering an enticing array of authentic flavors inspired by Mexico City. Led by Chef Doug Robson, Gallo Blanco is known for its fresh, flavorful ingredients and creative interpretations of traditional Mexican cuisine. The menu features an array of tacos, enchiladas, ceviches, and other mouthwatering delights that showcase the diverse regional tastes of Mexico. With a stylish and inviting ambiance, Gallo Blanco provides a perfect setting for a delicious and memorable dining experience, where guests can savor the vibrant colors and rich aromas of Mexican cuisine in the heart of Phoenix.

928 E Pierce St, Phoenix, AZ 85006

(602) 327-0880

Hours: Monday Closed; Tuesday-Friday 11 am-10 pm; Saturday 8 am-10 pm; Sunday 8 am-9 pm

www.galloblancocafe.com

Squid Ink Sushi Bar - $$

A modern sushi bar in Phoenix that captivates sushi enthusiasts with its innovative and artfully crafted dishes. Led by skilled chefs, the restaurant takes pride in using fresh, high-quality ingredients to create a delightful selection of sushi rolls and sashimi. Beyond traditional sushi, Squid Ink also offers creative fusion rolls that blend diverse flavors and textures. The chic and modern ambiance adds to the dining experience, making it a go-to spot for sushi aficionados and those looking to explore the world of Japanese cuisine. Squid Ink sushi bar promises a culinary journey of delectable flavors that leave patrons wanting more.

9947 W Happy Valley Pkwy #109, Peoria, AZ 85383

(623) 561-7747

Hours: Sunday-Thursday 11 am-9 pm; Friday-Saturday 11 am-11 pm

www.squidinksushi.com

The Wild Thaiger - $$

A popular Thai restaurant captivating diners with its authentic and flavorful Thai cuisine. With a menu inspired by the vibrant flavors of Thailand, the restaurant offers an array of traditional dishes, from classic Pad Thai and Green Curry to unique specialties like Tom Yum soup and Mango Sticky Rice. The Wild Thaiger's commitment to using fresh ingredients and bold spices ensures an unforgettable dining experience. The warm and inviting atmosphere adds to the charm, making it a favorite spot for locals and visitors seeking a taste of Thailand in the heart of Phoenix.

2631 N Central Ave, Phoenix, AZ 85004

(602) 241-8995

Hours: Monday-Friday 11 am-9 pm; Saturday 5 pm-9 pm; Sunday Closed

www.wildthaiger.com

Mekong Palace Chinese Restaurant - $$

Celebrated for its authentic and flavorful Chinese cuisine and specializing in Szechuan and Cantonese dishes, the restaurant offers a diverse menu that caters to various tastes and preferences. From mouthwatering stir-fries to delectable seafood dishes and their famous dim sum, Mekong Palace delivers a tantalizing experience that captures the essence of Chinese flavors. With its dedication to quality ingredients and skillful preparation, Mekong Palace continues to charm diners, offering an unforgettable taste of China in the heart of Phoenix.

66 S Dobson Rd ste 120, Mesa, AZ 85202

(480) 962-0493

Hours: Monday-Friday, 11 am-9 pm; Saturday-Sunday, 10 am-9 pm

www.mekongpalace.com

Tandoori Times Indian Bistro - $$

Known for its authentic and aromatic Indian cuisine, the restaurant offers a diverse menu that showcases a wide range of Indian delicacies, including flavorful tandoori dishes, rich curries, and biryanis. With a focus on using fresh, high-quality ingredients and traditional Indian spices, Tandoori Times delivers a culinary journey that satisfies Indian food enthusiasts and newcomers alike. The warm and inviting ambiance adds to the dining experience, making it a favorite spot for those seeking an unforgettable taste of India.

14891 N Northsight Blvd #119, Scottsdale, AZ 85260

(480) 794-1404

Hours fluctuate, so please visit the website to plan your dinner!

www.tandooritimes.com

Pita Jungle - $$

With 21 locations across Arizona, this Mediterranean-inspired restaurant offers a creative twist to the classic flavors. On the menu, you'll find a variety of dishes, including delicious pitas, salads, and hummus platters, all made with wholesome ingredients and bold Mediterranean flavors. Pita Jungle takes pride in catering to various dietary preferences, with vegetarian, vegan, and gluten-free options available. The laid-back yet vibrant ambiance makes it an ideal spot for friends and families to gather and enjoy a satisfying meal.

Since there are so many locations, you're bound to find one nearby. Visit the website for location details.
www.pitajungle.com

FARM TO TABLE

Quiessence at the Farm - $$$$

This hidden culinary gem highlighted at The Farm at South Mountain offers a farm-to-table, fine-dining experience, showcasing seasonal ingredients sourced from their own organic gardens and local farms. The menu is a blend of rustic and refined, featuring creative and flavorful dishes that celebrate the flavors of the Southwest. The serene and picturesque setting, surrounded by lush gardens and groves, adds to the intimate dining experience. Quiessence at the Farm offers a delightful escape from the hustle and bustle of the city, providing an authentic taste of Arizona's agricultural bounty.

6106 S 32nd St, Phoenix, AZ 85042

(602) 276-0601

Hours: Sunday, Monday & Wednesday Closed; Tuesday & Thursday 5 pm-8 pm; Friday & Saturday 5 pm-8:30 pm

www.qatthefarm.com

True Food Kitchen - $$

This is one of the few national chains you will find in this book; however, True Food Kitchen offers a genuine Farm to Table experience filled with fresh, nutritious, and flavorful ingredients. The menu features delicious dishes crafted to accommodate various dietary preferences, including vegan, vegetarian, and gluten-free options. With a commitment to serving locally sourced and sustainable ingredients, True Food Kitchen delivers on every course and cocktail. The modern,s inviting atmosphere and attentive service make it a popular choice for health-conscious diners seeking a vibrant and wholesome culinary experience.

   2502 E Camelback Rd Suite 135, Phoenix, AZ 85016

   (602) 774-3488

   Hours: Monday-Thursday 11 am-9 pm; Friday 11 am-10 pm; Saturday 10 am-10 pm; Sunday 10 am-9 pm

   www.truefoodkitchen.com/locations/phoenix

Blue Hound Kitchen & Cocktails - $$$

This chic restaurant and cocktail lounge in Downtown Phoenix offers a sophisticated dining experience. The menu features a creative blend of modern American cuisine with locally sourced and seasonal ingredients. Blue Hound's handcrafted cocktails are a highlight, complementing the culinary offerings perfectly. Since it's open for breakfast, lunch, and dinner, you're bound to find an opportunity to pop in. Be careful; they close for a quick break mid-morning around 10:30 am on weekdays!

   2 E Jefferson St, Phoenix, AZ 85004

   (602) 258-0231

   Hours: Monday-Thursday 6:30 am-11 pm; Friday 6:30 am-12a m; Saturday 8 am-12 am; Sunday 8 am-11 pm

   www.bluehoundkitchen.com

The Farm at South Mountain - $$

A picturesque oasis nestled in the heart of Phoenix, this charming destination offers a unique and idyllic escape from the city's hustle and bustle. The property features lush gardens, groves, and meandering paths, providing a serene setting for leisurely strolls and relaxation. Visitors can explore the organic gardens and dine at the renowned restaurants, Quiessence at the Farm and Morning Glory Café, which serve farm-fresh and flavorful dishes. With its peaceful ambiance and farm-to-table dining options, The Farm at South Mountain offers a delightful experience that celebrates nature's beauty and the land's bounty. The outdoor cafe closes during the summer due to extreme heat, so check the website for the most up-to-date hours during your stay.

6106 S 32nd St, Phoenix, AZ 85042

(602) 276-6360

www.thefarmatsouthmountain.com

Flower Child - $$

This a vibrant and health-conscious restaurant that celebrates wholesome and flavorful food. Harnessing the farm-to-table philosophy, their menu offers an array of delicious salads, bowls, wraps, and vegetable-forward dishes. Flower Child's commitment to catering to various dietary preferences, including vegan, vegetarian, and gluten-free options, makes it a popular choice for health-conscious diners. The relaxed and cheerful atmosphere creates a welcoming space for friends and families to enjoy a nourishing meal. Whether you're craving a nutrient-packed salad or a hearty grain bowl, Flower Child in Phoenix provides a delightful and nutritious dining experience.

Desert Ridge Marketplace

21001 N Tatum Blvd #16-1000, Phoenix, AZ 85050

(480) 397-5056

Uptown Plaza

100 E Camelback Rd, Phoenix, AZ 85012

(480) 212-0180

Camelback Village Center

5013 N 44th St, Phoenix, AZ 85018

(602) 429-6222

Hours: Monday-Sunday, 11 am-9 pm

www.iamaflowerchild.com

FINE DINING

Steak 44 - $$$$

Steak 44 is a premier steakhouse with a luxurious and unforgettable dining experience. With its elegant and upscale ambiance, the restaurant offers a perfect setting for special occasions and celebrations. The menu showcases a selection of top-quality, hand-cut steaks cooked to perfection and accompanied by delectable sides and decadent desserts. Alongside its renowned steaks, the restaurant also offers a variety of seafood and other chef-inspired dishes. The attentive service and extensive wine list enhance the overall dining experience. Steak 44's dedication to impeccable service and exceptional cuisine has earned it a reputation as one of Phoenix's finest steakhouses.

   5101 N 44th St, Phoenix, AZ 85018
   (602) 271-4400
   Hours: Sunday-Thursday 4 pm-10 pm; Friday & Saturday 4 pm-11 pm
   www.steak44.com

Binkley's Restaurant - $$$$

Led by renowned Chef Kevin Binkley, Binkley's is a highly acclaimed fine dining establishment in Phoenix. The restaurant offers an extraordinary culinary experience that blends innovation with classic flavors. The menu showcases a carefully curated selection of seasonally inspired dishes crafted with the finest ingredients and impeccable attention to detail. Binkley's is known for its ever-changing tasting menus, allowing guests to savor an array of imaginative and artfully presented dishes. The elegant and intimate setting, paired with personalized service, creates a memorable dining affair that has earned Binkley's Restaurant a reputation as one of Phoenix's premier dining destinations.

   2320 E Osborn Rd, Phoenix, AZ 85016
   (602) 388-4874
   Hours: Sunday-Tuesday Closed; Wednesday-Saturday 6:30 pm-10 pm
   www.binkleysrestaurant.com

Tarbell's - $$$

Founded by award-winning Chef Mark Tarbell, this renowned and long-standing restaurant is known for its sophisticated yet approachable American cuisine. Tarbell's showcases a menu that evolves with the seasons, emphasizing fresh and locally sourced ingredients. The restaurant is celebrated for its expertly prepared steaks, seafood, and innovative dishes highlighting Chef Tarbell's culinary expertise. The elegant and inviting ambiance and attentive service create a welcoming atmosphere for intimate dinners and special occasions.

3213 E Camelback Rd, Phoenix, AZ 85018
(602) 955-8100
Hours: Monday-Saturday 4 pm-10 pm; Sunday 4 pm-9 pm
www.tarbells.com

Different Pointe of View - $$$$

This is an upscale, iconic restaurant perched atop the scenic North Mountain, creating breathtaking views of the city and surrounding mountains. Led by Executive Chef Anthony DeMuro, the restaurant specializes in contemporary American cuisine with a focus on seasonal and locally sourced ingredients. Chef DeMuro's menu features an array of creative dishes complemented by an extensive wine list. The elegant and refined ambiance provides the perfect backdrop for a memorable dining experience. With its impeccable service and panoramic vistas, Different Pointe of View continues to captivate guests. It remains a coveted destination for special occasions and romantic dinners.

11111 N 7th St, Phoenix, AZ 85020
(602) 866-6350
Hours: Monday Closed; Tuesday-Sunday 5 pm-9 pm
www.tapatiocliffshilton.com/dining/different-pointe-of-view

Ocean Prime - $$$$

This contemporary, stylish seafood and steakhouse captures an elegant setting for fine dining and special occasions. The menu features a diverse selection of fresh seafood, prime cuts of steak, and other delectable dishes, all expertly prepared and presented. Ocean Prime's dedication to using high-quality ingredients and impeccable service creates a luxurious dining experience. The restaurant's commitment to excellence and attention to detail has earned it a reputation as one of Phoenix's premier dining destinations, drawing in discerning food enthusiasts across the city.

5455 E High St #115, Phoenix, AZ 85054

(480) 347-1313

Hours: Sunday-Thursday 4 pm-9 pm; Friday & Saturday 4 pm-10 pm

www.ocean-prime.com/locations-menus/phoenix

CRAFT BEER & LOCAL WINE

O.H.S.O Brewery & Distillery - $$

Known for its handcrafted beers and spirits, this is a popular destination for locals. With a focus on sustainability, the brewery uses locally sourced ingredients to create a diverse selection of flavorful craft beers and creative cocktails. The spacious and inviting atmosphere, with its dog-friendly patio, offers a relaxed and welcoming environment for friends and families to gather and enjoy delicious drinks and bites. O.H.S.O Brewery & Distillery's commitment to innovation has made it a favorite spot for beer and spirits enthusiasts, providing a unique and memorable dining and drinking experience.

Paradise Valley

10810 N Tatum Blvd #126, Phoenix, AZ 85028

(602) 900-9003

Hours: Monday-Thursday 11 am-10 pm; Friday 11 am-12 am; Saturday 9 am-12 am; Sunday 9 am-10 pm

Scottsdale

4900 E Indian School Rd, Phoenix, AZ 85018

(602) 955-0358

Hours: Monday-Thursday 11 am-10 pm; Friday 11 am-12 am; Saturday 9 am-12 am; Sunday 9 am-10 pm

North Scottsdale

15681 N Hayden Rd # 112, Scottsdale, AZ 85260

(480) 948-3159

Hours: Monday-Friday, 11 am-10 pm; Saturday & Sunday, 9 am-10 pm

https://www.ohsobrewery.com/

Turquoise Wine Cellar and Tasting Room - $$

This charming and intimate wine bar is dedicated to showcasing a curated selection of exceptional wines. The cellar offers an array of both local and international wines carefully chosen by knowledgeable sommeliers. With its cozy and welcoming ambiance, the tasting room provides a perfect setting for wine enthusiasts to explore new varietals and enjoy expertly crafted wine flights. The knowledgeable staff is always ready to offer recommendations and share insights, enhancing the overall tasting experience. Turquoise Wine Cellar and Tasting Room is a hidden gem, offering a delightful escape for wine lovers.

8160 W Union Hills Dr #B200, Glendale, AZ 85308

(480) 859-2788

Hours: Monday Closed; Tuesday-Thursday 12 pm-8 pm; Friday & Saturday 12 pm-9 pm; Sunday 12 pm-5 pm

www.turquoisewinebar.com

Huss Brewing Co - $$

With multiple locations across the valley, Huss Brewing Co is renowned for its high-quality beers and innovative brews. Founded by Jeff and Leah Huss, the brewery offers a diverse selection of handcrafted beers, ranging from classic ales and lagers to creative and experimental brews. Huss Brewing Co is committed to using locally sourced ingredients, thus capturing the essence of Arizona in every sip. The brewery's friendly and vibrant taproom and spacious patio provide a welcoming space for beer enthusiasts to enjoy delicious brews and experience the thriving craft beer scene in

Phoenix

Uptown Plaza

100 E Camelback Rd #160, Phoenix, AZ 85012

(602) 441-4677

Hours: Sunday Closed; Monday-Thursday 3 pm-8 pm; Friday & Saturday 11 am-9 pm

Phoenix Convention Center

225 E Monroe St, Phoenix, AZ 85004

(602) 607-5370

Hours: Sunday-Thursday 11 am-9 pm; Friday & Saturday 11 am-10 pm

Tempe

1520 W Mineral Rd # 102, Tempe, AZ 85283

(480) 264-7611

Hours: Monday-Thursday 3 pm-8 pm; Friday 3 pm-10 pm; Saturday 12 pm-8 pm; Sunday 12 pm-6 pm

www.hussbrewing.com

Pedal Haus Brewery - $$

Pedal Haus Brewery is popular and also has multiple locations around Phoenix. Known for its handcrafted beers and vibrant atmosphere, the brewery has a wide range of beer styles, from traditional ales to creative and experimental brews. With a passion for craft beer and a commitment to quality, Pedal Haus delivers an exceptional tasting experience for beer enthusiasts. The brewery's spacious indoor and outdoor seating areas and its delicious food menu create the ideal setting for friends and families to gather and enjoy a memorable time together. Pedal Haus Brewery has become a favorite destination for locals and visitors seeking a taste of Arizona's craft beer culture.

Tempe

730 S Mill Ave #102, Tempe, AZ 85281

(480) 314-2337

Hours: Monday-Thursday 11 am-11 pm; Friday & Saturday 11 am-1 am; Sunday 11 am-10 pm

Phoenix

214 E Roosevelt St, Suite 4, Phoenix, AZ 85004

(623) 213-8229

Hours: Monday-Thursday 3 pm-10 pm; Friday 3 pm-12 am; Saturday 10 am-12 am; Sunday 10 am-10 pm

Chandler

95 W Boston St, Chandler, AZ 85225

(480) 656-1639

Hours: Monday & Tuesday 3 pm-10 pm; Wednesday & Thursday 11 am-10 pm; Friday & Saturday 11 am-12 am; Sunday 10 am-9 pm

www.pedalhausbrewery.com

Arizona Stronghold Vineyards - $$

Arizona's most prominent winery, based in Cottonwood, AZ, is dedicated to producing exceptional wines that showcase the unique terroir of Arizona. Founded by renowned winemakers Eric Glomski and Maynard James Keenan, the vineyard focuses on sustainability and organic practices to cultivate the best grapes. Their diverse wine portfolio offers a range of varietals, from crisp whites to bold reds, reflecting the distinct characteristics of the region's soil and climate. With a passion for winemaking and a commitment to quality, Arizona Stronghold Vineyards has become a celebrated destination for wine enthusiasts looking to experience the vibrant flavors of Arizona's wine country.

Old Town Scottsdale's Tasting Room

4225 N Marshall Way Suite #2, Scottsdale, AZ 85251

(480) 779-1600

Hours: Monday-Wednesday Closed; Sunday & Thursday 1 pm-7 pm; Friday & Saturday 12 pm-8:30 pm www.azstronghold.com

FOOD TRUCKS

AZ Festivals

AZ Feastivals is a collective of food truck events held at various locations across Arizona, offering a unique and exciting dining experience. Currently, in Gilbert, Queen Creek, and Mesa, these festivals showcase diverse culinary delights from food trucks specializing in various cuisines. AZ Festivals have something to please every palate, whether you're craving savory street food, gourmet burgers, mouthwatering tacos, or sweet treats. With live music, family-friendly activities, and a festive atmosphere, these events create a perfect opportunity for friends and families to come together, savor delicious food, and enjoy a memorable time in Arizona's vibrant food truck culture. Please visit the website for new or altered event locations!

www.azfeastivals.com/weekly-festivals
(480) 599-0207

Queen Creek Library
21802 S Ellsworth Rd, Queen Creek, AZ 85142
Fridays 5:30-9 pm
www.facebook.com/queencreekfeastival

Gilbert Heritage District
222 N. Gilbert Rd. Gilbert AZ 85234
Fridays 5:30-9 pm
www.facebook.com/GilbertFeastival

Mesa Pioneer Park
526 E Main St. Mesa, AZ 85203
Saturdays 5 pm-9 pm
www.facebook.com/MesaFeastival

Ahwatukee Eats

Another Friday event is the Ahwatukee Eats in the Ahwatukee Foothills. This event brings together a variety of local restaurants and food vendors, offering a delicious showcase of the area's culinary talent. From traditional favorites to international flavors, Ahwatukee Eats allows visitors to indulge in mouthwatering dishes of every kind. The event's lively and community-oriented atmosphere makes it a wonderful outing for families and friends to enjoy great food, live entertainment, and camaraderie. Ahwatukee Eats celebrates the rich culinary diversity of the neighborhood, making it a must-visit for food enthusiasts in Phoenix. This event usually shuts down during the summer, so please check the Facebook page for the most up-to-date availability.

4609 E Chandler Blvd. Phoenix, AZ 85048

(424) 675-1563

www.facebook.com/ahwatukeeeats

Food Truck Friday West

Every Friday evening, food truck vendors from various cuisines gather to offer a delectable selection of dishes. From gourmet burgers to mouthwatering tacos, sweet treats, and more, there's something to please every palate. The event's vibrant atmosphere, live music, and family-friendly activities create a fun experience for visitors of all ages. Food Truck Friday West provides the perfect chance to taste a plethora of delicious eats and enjoy a delightful evening out in the heart of Glendale. The hours and location vary during the summer, so check the website during your trip. The website details which trucks will attend that week, so every visit will always be different!

getlocalarizonaevents.com/foodtruckfridaywest

First Friday West Valley

This lively and vibrant community event lights up the town on the first Friday of each month in Tolleson. It's family-friendly and celebrates local art, culture, and food in the lower West Valley. Visitors can explore the works of talented artists and artisans, enjoy live music and entertainment, and savor delicious offerings from food vendors and trucks. The event's welcoming and inclusive atmosphere fosters a sense of community and showcases Tolleson's diverse and creative spirit. First Friday West Valley is a must-visit for locals and visitors looking to experience the unique cultural scene of this charming city. Times 2 Entertainment hosts several significant events around the Valley, so visit the Facebook page to see if another event is nearby.

Whyman Park
2350 S. 103rd Ave. Tolleson, AZ 85353
(480) 406-1200
www.facebook.com/Times2Entertainment/events

KID-FRIENDLY

Morning Squeeze - $$

This kid-friendly eatery promises a fun and delightful dining experience for families. The vibrant and colorful decor, along with playful menu items, captures the attention of young diners. From pancake stacks to breakfast burritos, the menu offers a variety of kid-approved dishes that cater to different taste buds. The restaurant's friendly staff and welcoming ambiance create a warm and inviting atmosphere for families to enjoy a delicious breakfast or brunch together. Whether it's a weekend treat or a special occasion, Morning Squeeze is the perfect spot for families to start their day with smiles and laughter.

Phoenix
1 N 1st St #100, Phoenix, AZ 85004
(602) 675-2641

Scottsdale
4233 N Scottsdale Rd, Scottsdale, AZ 85251
(480) 945-4669

Tempe
690 S Mill Ave #110, Tempe, AZ 85281
(480) 264-4688
Hours: Monday-Sunday 7 am-2 pm
morningsqueeze.com/tempe

Someburros - $

Another kid-friendly option is the Mexican restaurant Someburros with multiple locations in Phoenix. The restaurant offers a casual and inviting atmosphere, making it a popular choice for families. The kid's menu features tasty and authentic Mexican dishes tailored to children's preferences. From kid-sized burritos to quesadillas and tacos, there are plenty of options to satisfy young appetites. Someburros is known for its friendly service and casual ambiance, providing a comfortable space for families with a stress-free dining experience. With its tasty food and family-friendly environment, Someburros is a favorite destination for parents and kids alike.

Goodyear
50 N Estrella Pkwy, Goodyear, AZ 85338
(623) 440-6882

Phoenix
5115 N 7th St, Phoenix, AZ 85014
(602) 584-8226

Tempe
1314 S Rural Rd, Tempe, AZ 85281
(480) 446-8226
Hours: Sunday-Thursday 9 am-9 pm; Friday & Saturday 9 am-10 pm
www.someburros.com

Chelsea's Kitchen - $$

This restaurant features a diverse menu with dishes that appeal to adults and children. The kid's menu offers delicious options like mini burgers, chicken tenders, and macaroni and cheese, ensuring that young diners will find something they love. Chelsea's Kitchen also provides coloring sheets and crayons for kids, keeping them entertained while waiting for their meals. Chelsea's Kitchen is a great choice for families with its kid-friendly menu and family-oriented atmosphere.

  5040 N 40th St, Phoenix, AZ 85018

  (602) 957-2555

  www.chelseaskitchenaz.com

Ruslter's Rooste - $$

This restaurant is designed to resemble an old Western town, complete with cowboy decor and a slide that leads into the dining area. The kid's menu offers a range of tasty and familiar dishes, including burgers, chicken tenders, and spaghetti. Rustler's Rooste also provides coloring sheets and cowboy hats for young diners, adding to the playful and entertaining experience. With its unique atmosphere and delicious food, Rustler's Rooste is a hit among families looking for a memorable dining adventure in Phoenix.

  8383 S 48th St, Phoenix, AZ 85044

  (602) 431-6474

  Hours: Monday-Thursday 5 pm-9 pm; Friday 5 pm-10 pm; Saturday 4:30 pm-9 pm; Sunday 4:30 pm-9 pm

  www.rustlersrooste.com

Luci's at the Orchard - $$

This restaurant features a welcoming and relaxed atmosphere with a spacious outdoor patio complete with a mini splash zone, so be prepared for a damp ride home. The kid's menu offers a variety of tasty and wholesome options, from pancakes and French toast for breakfast to sandwiches and macaroni and cheese for lunch. Luci's at the Orchard also has a great selection of desserts and treats that kids will love.

  7100 N 12th St building 2, Phoenix, AZ 85020

(602) 633-2442
Hours: Sunday-Tuesday 7 am-3 pm; Wednesday-Saturday 7 am-8 pm
www.lucisgoodness.com

PATIOS AND ROOFTOPS

Culinary Dropout - $$

Known for its eclectic and creative menu, this restaurant's chic and modern ambiance creates a vibrant and fashionable dining experience. The menu boasts diverse dishes, from gourmet burgers to inventive salads and flavorful entrees. Culinary Dropout also boasts an extensive selection of craft beers, cocktails, and wines, making it a hotspot for socializing and enjoying a night out with friends. Culinary Dropout is a go-to destination with its modern vibe, delectable food, and trendy atmosphere.

Phoenix
5632 N 7th St, Phoenix, AZ 85014
(602) 680-4040
Hours: Monday-Thursday 11 am-10 pm; Friday 11 am-12 am; Saturday 10 am-12 am; Sunday 10 am-9 pm

Tempe
149 S Farmer Ave, Tempe, AZ 85281
(480) 240-1601
Hours: Monday-Thursday 11 am-10 pm; Friday 11 am-1 am; Saturday 10 am-1 am; Sunday 10 am-10 pm

Scottsdale Waterfront
7135 E Camelback Rd #125, Scottsdale, AZ 85251
(480) 970-1700
Hours: Monday-Thursday 11 am-10 pm; Friday 11 am-12 am; Saturday 10 am-12 am; Sunday 10 am-9 pm
www.culinarydropout.com

The Churchill - $$

Situated at the core of Roosevelt Row, the dynamic Artist's District in Downtown Phoenix, The Churchill is a hub of local culture and community engagement. This patio-inspired space hosts ten small businesses: The Brill Line, Infruition, So Far So Good, Loco Style Grindz, Freak Brothers, Scookie Bar, State Forty-Eight, Stoop Kid, Cayla Gray, & Neighbor Market. The venue artfully merges food, beverages, and retail offerings with arts, music, and community events. Embracing an urban development concept, The Churchill's shared courtyard fosters connections among locals and injects creative experiences into the already thriving neighborhood. It serves as a compelling destination where the community can immerse themselves in the vibrant spirit of Phoenix's artistic and culinary scene.

901 N 1st St, Phoenix, AZ 85004

Hours: Monday Closed; Tuesday, Wednesday & Sunday 10 am-10 pm; Thursday 10 am-12 am; Friday & Saturday 10 am-1:30 am

www.thechurchillphx.com

Eden Rooftop Bar - $$

Located atop The Camby Hotel, this trendy bar provides stunning views of the Phoenix skyline and the surrounding mountains. The ambiance is modern and elegant, with a laid-back yet upscale vibe. Guests can enjoy an extensive selection of craft cocktails, wines, and beers, complemented by a menu featuring delicious bites and small plates. Whether it's a sunset drink with friends or a romantic evening under the stars, Eden Rooftop Bar offers an unforgettable setting for those seeking a luxurious and elevated rooftop experience in Phoenix.

2 E Jefferson St, Phoenix, AZ 85004

(602) 258-0231

Hours: Sunday-Wednesday 11 am-9 pm; Thursday- Saturday 11 am-12 am

www.edenbarphoenix.com

Upstairs at Flint - $$$

Perched above the upscale restaurant Flint by Baltaire, this hidden gem offers a relaxed and intimate setting. Guests can unwind on the rooftop terrace while enjoying picturesque views of the cityscape and Arizona sunsets. The bar features a curated selection of handcrafted cocktails, premium wines, and local beers. With its warm and welcoming atmosphere, Upstairs at Flint provides the perfect spot for a leisurely drink with friends or a romantic evening. It's a must-visit destination for those seeking a sophisticated rooftop experience in Phoenix.

2425 E Camelback Rd, Phoenix, AZ 85016

(602) 812-4818

Hours: Sunday-Wednesday Closed; Thursday-Saturday 6 pm-10 pm

www.flintbybaltaire.com/upstairs-at-flint

Hash Kitchen & The Sicilian Butcher - $$

Located in the vibrant Park West shopping center, the same husband and wife team owns these two seemingly unrelated restaurants. At Hash Kitchen, guests can choose from a diverse menu featuring a wide array of hash creations, benedicts, and pancakes. It is well-known for its build-your-own Bloody Mary bar and Mimosa Flights. At The Sicilian Butcher, the menu showcases a variety of handcrafted pasta, mouthwatering meatballs, and other traditional Italian delicacies made with the freshest ingredients. Another highlight is The Sicilian Baker inside the restaurant offering traditional desserts to eat after your meal or to take home to a party. All this to say, their shared patio is incredibly spacious and a perfect outdoor setting for a delicious meal, no matter what you're in the mood for.

The Sicilian Butcher/Baker

15530 N Tatum Blvd #160, Phoenix, AZ 85032

(602) 775-5140

Hours: Sunday-Thursday 11 am-10 pm; Friday & Saturday 11 am-10:30 pm

www.thesicilianbutcher.com

Hash Kitchen

RESTAURANTS, BARS, & BAKERIES

9780 W Northern Ave Suite 1110, Peoria, AZ 85345

(623) 471-5471

Hours: Monday-Friday, 7 am-2 pm; Saturday & Sunday, 7 am-3 pm

www.hashkitchen.com

DESSERTS & BAKERIES

The Boyer Bakery

Known for its artisanal and freshly baked treats, this charming bakery offers a warm and cozy atmosphere, making it a perfect spot for a morning pastry and a cup of coffee or an afternoon indulgence. The menu features creations like a Cookie Butter Smore Bar, a Brookie Dough Bar, their version of a Pop-Tart, & a Banana Creme Pie Cookie. Boyer Bakery caters to every sweet craving, from flaky croissants to decadent chocolate cakes. The case varies daily with whatever catches the chef's whim and will sell out by the end of the day! Whether a quick grab-and-go treat or a leisurely sit-down experience, Boyer Bakery promises a delightful sugar-filled experience!

13681 N Litchfield Rd, Surprise, AZ 85379

Hours: Sunday & Monday Closed; Tuesday-Friday 6 am-3 pm; Saturday 8 am-3 pm

www.theboyerbakery.com

The Yard Milkshake Bar

This a whimsical and indulgent dessert destination offering over-the-top milkshakes and delectable treats. Located in the bustling District at Desert Ridge Marketplace, this popular spot is known for its extravagant and creatively crafted milkshakes. Guests can choose from various mouthwatering flavors and toppings, creating their dream milkshake masterpiece. The Yard Milkshake Bar also offers other sweet treats like cookie dough scoops, edible cookie dough bowls, and ice cream sandwiches. With its fun and playful ambiance, The Yard Milkshake Bar is the perfect spot for dessert lovers looking to satisfy their sweet tooth in style.

50 W Jefferson St, Phoenix, AZ 85004

(602) 296-4473

Hours: Sunday-Wednesday 12 pm-9 pm; Thursday-Saturday 12 pm-10 pm

www.theyardmilkshakebar.com

The Beignet Babe

The Beignet Babe food truck is this section's most elusive dessert shop. Specializing in delectable New Orleans-style beignets, this charming truck brings the taste of the French Quarter to the streets of Phoenix, serving up freshly fried, pillowy beignets dusted with powdered sugar. Guests can indulge in these delightful treats at local events, festivals, and gatherings, experiencing the sweet and authentic flavors of New Orleans right in their own backyard. The Beignet Babe food truck's warm and friendly staff and irresistible beignets make it a must-try destination for those seeking a taste of the Big Easy in the heart of Arizona. Check out their website to see when they'll be at a festival near you!

(602) 881-5683

www.beignetbabe.shop

Urban Cookies Bakeshop

Renowned for its gourmet cookies and sweet treats, this charming bakeshop offers a cozy and inviting atmosphere making it the perfect spot to indulge in freshly baked goodies. Their delectable cookies, made from scratch with high-quality ingredients, come in a variety of flavors, from classic chocolate chips to unique creations like lavender shortbread. They also serve gorgeous cupcakes, brownies, and other sweet delights.

2325 N 7th St, Phoenix, AZ 85006

(602) 451-4335

Hours: Sunday Closed; Monday-Friday 8 am-6 pm; Saturday 8 am-5 pm

RESTAURANTS, BARS, & BAKERIES

www.urbancookies.com

Voodoo Doughnut

Originating in Portland, Oregon, this one-of-a-kind doughnut destination is known for its innovative and outrageous flavors, creative designs, and eclectic decor. Guests can delight in a sugary swirl of unique donut creations, from the famous Voodoo Doll donut to the Bacon Maple Bar and vegan options. With its vibrant and whimsical atmosphere, Voodoo Doughnut offers a fun and memorable experience for donut enthusiasts and foodies. The first Arizona location is scheduled to open in Tempe by the end of summer 2023, so check the website for the new store hours!
 1324 S Rural Rd, Tempe, AZ 85281
 (602) 641-6669
 www.voodoodoughnut.com

COFFEE SHOPS

Ebb & Flow Coffee Co.

This cozy and inviting space offers a relaxed and welcoming atmosphere to enjoy expertly brewed coffee or tea. Ebb & Flow takes pride in sourcing high-quality beans and offering a variety of coffee brewing methods to satisfy every palate. With a focus on sustainability and community, this coffee shop also hosts events and workshops to engage with the local community. Whether a quick morning pick-me-up or a leisurely afternoon coffee break, Ebb & Flow Coffee Co promises a delightful experience for coffee aficionados.
 21084 W Main St Ste 101, Buckeye, AZ 85396
 (623) 476-2348
 Hours: Monday-Sunday 6 am-3 pm
 19425 W Indian School Rd #101, Litchfield Park, AZ 85340
 (623) 259-9393

Hours: Monday-Sunday 6 am-7 pm
www.facebook.com/ebbandflowcoffeeco

Bad Ass Coffee of Hawaii

Inspired by the Hawaiian coffee culture, this laid-back and welcoming cafe serves a selection of premium 100% Kona coffee and other Hawaiian blends. Guests can savor a variety of handcrafted espresso drinks, cold brews, and Hawaiian specialties, like the famous Macadamia Nut Latte. With its island-inspired decor and friendly service, Bad Ass Coffee of Hawaii creates a relaxing and enjoyable atmosphere for coffee lovers to experience a little piece of Hawaii in the desert.

8363 W Van Buren St, Tolleson, AZ 85353
(480) 645-9064
Hours: Monday-Friday, 6 am-6 pm; Saturday & Sunday, 8 am-5 pm
50 W Jefferson St Suite 170, Phoenix, AZ 85003
(602) 388-4849
Hours: Monday-Friday, 6 am-6 pm; Saturday & Sunday, 7 am-5 pm
www.badasscoffee.com

Driftwood Coffee Co.

This boutique-style cafe is known for its specialty coffee and artisanal drinks. They source high-quality beans worldwide and expertly craft each cup perfectly. With a focus on sustainability, Driftwood Coffee Co offers a cozy and eco-friendly ambiance, making it a perfect spot for coffee enthusiasts and those looking to enjoy a relaxing atmosphere. Whether it's a classic espresso or a unique coffee creation, visitors can expect a delightful experience.

8295 W Jefferson St #6514, Peoria, AZ 85345
(602) 756-9051
Hours: Monday-Sunday 7 am-9 pm
www.driftwoodaz.com

The Human Bean

The Human Bean has gained a loyal following as a local drive-through Java joint. They source their beans from the best coffee-growing regions and offer specialty drinks, from classic lattes and mochas to unique flavored concoctions. The convenience of their drive-thru setup allows customers to grab a quick caffeine fix on the go. With its friendly baristas and high-quality beverages, The Human Bean is a go-to spot for coffee lovers.

1547 N Dysart Rd, Avondale, AZ 85392
(602) 860-2016
6502 N 16th St, Phoenix, AZ 85016
(602) 368-6391
2010 E Indian School Rd, Phoenix, AZ 85016
(602) 296-5466
20055 N 19th Ave, Phoenix, AZ 85027
(623) 440-4410
4377 E Baseline Rd, Phoenix, AZ 85042
(602) 296-7748
Hours: Monday-Friday, 5 am-7 pm; Saturday & Sunday, 6 am-7 pm
www.thehumanbean.com

Renegade Coffee Co.

This trendy and innovative coffee shop prides itself on living outside the boundaries of traditional coffee. With a passion for sustainability and unique flavors, Renegade Coffee Co sources ethically traded beans from local roasters and carefully crafts each cup to perfection. Their menu features a variety of handcrafted espresso drinks, pour-overs, cold brews, and creative signature beverages.

5959 N Granite Reef Rd, Scottsdale, AZ 85250
(480) 809-6284
1242 W University Dr, Mesa, AZ 85201
(480) 833-1930

Hours: Monday-Friday 6 am-6 pm; Saturday & Sunday 6:30 am-5:30 pm
www.renegadecoffeeaz.com

7

Day Trips

Sedona

Visiting Sedona is like traveling to a magical and awe-inspiring world of natural beauty. Surrounded by the magical red rock formations of the Coconino National Forest, Sedona offers a unique and enchanting experience for travelers seeking both relaxation and adventure.

The breathtaking landscape of Sedona provides countless opportunities for outdoor activities. Hiking enthusiasts can explore the numerous trails that wind through the red rocks, offering panoramic views of the surrounding area. Popular trails include Cathedral Rock, Devil's Bridge, and Bell Rock.

For a more leisurely experience, visitors can take scenic drives through Oak Creek Canyon or enjoy a peaceful picnic by the creek. Sedona is also known for its vortex sites, believed to be places of powerful energy and spiritual significance, making it a popular destination for wellness seekers and spiritual travelers.

In addition to its natural wonders, Sedona is a haven for art lovers and shoppers. The city has numerous art galleries and boutiques offering unique and handcrafted items, including Native American art and jewelry.

For a taste of the local cuisine, visitors can dine at charming restaurants or cafes that serve fresh and organic ingredients, often with a focus on

Southwestern flavors.

As the day comes to a close, Sedona's clear skies provide a perfect setting for stargazing, making it an excellent spot for astronomers and those seeking a peaceful evening under the stars.

Whether you're seeking adventure, relaxation, or a spiritual journey, Sedona's mystical landscape and serene ambiance offer an unforgettable experience that will leave you with cherished memories of this captivating Arizona gem.

Distance from Phoenix: 116 miles (about 2 hours driving)

Jerome

This charming and quirky mining town is atop Cleopatra Hill. This historic town, once a bustling copper mining hub, now offers travelers a unique and eclectic experience.

Perched on the side of Mingus Mountain, Jerome's winding streets are lined with beautifully preserved buildings from the past, now housing art galleries, boutiques, antique shops, and restaurants. Visitors can explore the town on foot, enjoying the old-world charm and stunning views of the Verde Valley below.

Jerome is renowned for its artistic community, and enthusiasts will find a vibrant art scene with many local artists showcasing their works. The town's lively music scene is also a draw for music lovers, with various live performances and events happening throughout the year.

For history buffs, the Jerome State Historic Park and the Mine Museum offer a glimpse into the town's mining past, complete with guided tours and exhibits illustrating the mining era's challenges and triumphs.

A visit to Jerome isn't complete without stopping at one of the many unique and quirky attractions, such as the Sliding Jail, where the town's jailhouse once slid down the hill, or the Haunted Hamburger restaurant, which boasts stunning views and spooky folklore.

Wine tasting is a delightful experience that takes you on a journey through the scenic Verde Valley vineyards. This charming mountain town is home to several wineries, each offering a unique selection of locally produced wines. Visitors can savor a variety of reds, whites, and rosés while enjoying stunning views of the surrounding landscape. Many wineries in Jerome also feature tasting rooms with knowledgeable staff who guide guests through the tasting process, providing insights into the winemaking process and the region's terroir.

Jerome's rich history, artistic charm, and breathtaking vistas make it a captivating destination for travelers seeking a one-of-a-kind experience in the heart of Arizona's mining country.

Distance from Phoenix: 111 miles (about 2 hours driving)

Bisbee

Another historic mining town that retains its old-world charm is in the Mule Mountains. It offers a unique and captivating experience for travelers seeking history, art, and natural beauty.

The town's colorful and well-preserved Victorian buildings house art galleries, boutiques, and restaurants. Strolling through the narrow streets, visitors can explore the town's rich mining history, evident in attractions like the Bisbee Mining & Historical Museum and the Queen Mine Tour, where they can venture into an actual former mine.

Bisbee is also known for its thriving arts scene, with many local artists calling the town home. Art enthusiasts can browse the numerous galleries, showcasing everything from paintings to sculptures.

Nature lovers will appreciate Bisbee's scenic beauty, with opportunities for hiking, birdwatching, and exploring the nearby canyons and caverns. The nearby Chiricahua National Monument and Coronado National Forest provide even more opportunities for outdoor adventures.

For a taste of local cuisine and culture, visitors can dine at the town's eclectic restaurants and cafes, offering a variety of delicious dishes, including Mexican and Southwestern flavors.

Bisbee's friendly and welcoming atmosphere is further highlighted by its festivals and events throughout the year, including the Bisbee Blues Festival and the Bisbee 1000 - The Great Stair Climb, which celebrates the town's unique architecture.

At the end of the day, visitors can relax in one of Bisbee's charming bed and breakfasts or boutique hotels, soaking in the atmosphere of this enchanting and quirky town.

Distance from Phoenix: 207 miles (about 3.25 hours driving)

Flagstaff

Escape to this charming mountain town surrounded by natural wonders. Situated at an elevation of 7,000 feet in the Coconino National Forest, Flagstaff offers a refreshing retreat from the desert heat and a diverse range of activities for travelers.

Outdoor enthusiasts will find adventures galore, with the nearby San Francisco Peaks providing hiking and mountain biking opportunities. The Lowell Observatory, famous for its astronomical discoveries, offers visitors a chance to explore the night sky through powerful telescopes.

Flagstaff's historic downtown is filled with quaint shops, galleries, and restaurants, reflecting the town's unique blend of Native American, Hispanic, and pioneer heritage. The vibrant arts and cultural scene includes numerous festivals and events showcasing local talent and traditions.

In addition to its natural beauty, Flagstaff is known for its commitment to sustainability and being a designated International Dark Sky City, offering breathtaking stargazing opportunities.

For those seeking a taste of the local brews, Flagstaff is home to a thriving craft beer scene with several breweries offering unique and flavorful concoctions.

Skiing in Flagstaff is a thrilling experience for those missing a snowy experience. The Arizona Snowbowl, located just minutes from downtown Flagstaff, provides skiers and snowboarders with excellent snow conditions and stunning views of the surrounding countryside, including the iconic San Francisco Peaks.

Distance from Phoenix: 144 miles (about 2.25 hours driving)

The Grand Canyon

Visiting the Grand Canyon is an awe-inspiring journey into the heart of one of the world's most magnificent natural wonders. Located in northern Arizona, this iconic landmark draws millions of visitors annually with its breathtaking beauty and vastness.

The Grand Canyon's sheer size and intricate layers of colorful rock formations tell a captivating geological story that spans millions of years. The South Rim, open year-round, offers numerous vantage points and viewpoints where visitors can marvel at the vast expanse and catch breathtaking sunrise and sunset views. For a more secluded experience, the less-visited North Rim provides a quieter and more rugged perspective.

For those outdoor enthusiasts, there are a wealth of activities, from hiking the rim trails to more challenging treks below the canyon's rim. The Bright Angel and South Kaibab Trails are popular for day hikes, while overnight backpacking trips offer a chance to explore the canyon's deeper regions.

For a unique perspective, helicopter and airplane tours allow visitors to soar over the canyon, revealing its grandeur from a bird's-eye view.

The Grand Canyon's rich cultural history is also on display, with several historic buildings and Native American ruins found throughout the area. The nearby Grand Canyon Village offers visitor centers, museums, and shops where guests can learn more about the canyon's natural and human history.

Stargazing at the Grand Canyon is an unforgettable experience, as its remote location and lack of light pollution create a perfect canvas for admiring the night sky.

Distance from Phoenix: 229 miles (about 3.5 hours driving)

Tombstone

Take a step back in time to the Wild West era. Known as "The Town Too Tough to Die," Tombstone preserves its rich history and legends of the Old West, making it a captivating destination for history enthusiasts and curious travelers.

The main attraction is the historic district, where visitors can explore the iconic Allen Street, lined with saloons, shops, and old-timey photo studios. The O.K. Corral is a must-see, famous for the gunfight between the Earp brothers and the Clanton-McLaury gang. Daily reenactments bring this legendary event to life.

Tombstone is also home to numerous historic buildings, museums, and guided tours that showcase the town's fascinating past. The Bird Cage Theatre, once a raucous saloon and theater, now offers ghost tours and a glimpse into the rough and tumble past.

In addition to its historical attractions, Tombstone hosts annual events and festivals celebrating its Western heritage, such as the Helldorado Days and Wyatt Earp Days.

The town's atmosphere is enhanced by locals dressed in period costumes and horse-drawn carriages, creating an immersive experience reminiscent of the 1880s.

Surrounded by the beautiful Sonoran Desert, Tombstone offers outdoor activities like horseback riding, hiking, and scenic drives.

Whether exploring the storied streets, witnessing gunfight reenactments, or simply soaking in the Wild West ambiance, a visit to Tombstone promises an unforgettable journey into the past and an appreciation for the frontier spirit that shaped this legendary town.

Distance from Phoenix: 184 miles (about 3 hours driving)

Rocky Point, Mexico

Rocky Point, also known as Puerto Peñasco, is a delightful getaway on the Sea of Cortez for those missing the beach. This popular vacation destination offers a mix of sun, sea, and sand, making it an ideal spot for relaxation and outdoor adventure.

Rocky Point boasts beautiful sandy beaches, clear turquoise waters, and a wide range of water activities. There are plenty of ways to enjoy the ocean: swimming, snorkeling, jet skiing, and paddleboarding.

The area is also known for its vibrant marine life, making it an excellent spot for whale watching and fishing charters. During the right season, visitors may even spot pods of dolphins playing in the waves.

For those seeking a bit of culture, the Old Port area offers charming shops, restaurants, and local art galleries. Take the chance to savor fresh seafood dishes and traditional Mexican cuisine at the numerous beachfront restaurants.

Adventurers can explore the nearby desert landscape on ATV tours or visit El Pinacate Biosphere Reserve, a UNESCO World Heritage site known for its unique volcanic landscapes and diverse wildlife.

Distance from Phoenix: 212 miles (about 4 hours driving)

*This is crossing the border into Mexico, so be prepared with a Passport and any customs rules and regulations.

8

Practical Information & Resources

TRANSPORTATION

Public Transportation - ValleyMetro.org

Valley Metro Rail

Operating since December 2008, this modern and efficient rail network spans 28 miles and connects major areas like Phoenix, Tempe, and Mesa. With 38 stations along its route, the Valley Metro Rail provides convenient and reliable transportation for residents and visitors.

The light rail's alignment is strategically designed to connect essential destinations, including downtown Phoenix, Arizona State University's Tempe campus, and the Mesa Arts Center. This connectivity makes it a popular choice for commuters, students, and tourists looking to explore the region.

The Valley Metro Rail offers frequent service, ensuring minimal wait times for passengers. Its trains are equipped with modern amenities such as air conditioning and onboard Wi-Fi, providing a comfortable and enjoyable travel experience.

In addition to its convenience, the Valley Metro Rail contributes to reducing traffic congestion and promoting eco-friendly transportation options in the metropolitan area. By encouraging public transit usage, the rail system plays a crucial role in the city's efforts to address environmental challenges.

The success of the Valley Metro Rail has spurred further expansion plans, with ongoing projects to extend the network and enhance connectivity to other parts of the metro area. As the Valley of the Sun grows, the light rail system remains an integral part of its public transportation infrastructure, offering a cost-effective and sustainable mode of travel for locals and tourists alike.

Phoenix Transit Bus

The bus is a vital component of the city's public transportation network, offering a comprehensive and accessible way for residents and visitors to get around. Operated by Valley Metro, the bus system covers an extensive network of routes, connecting various neighborhoods, shopping centers, educational institutions, and popular attractions throughout the metropolitan area.

The Phoenix Transit Bus fleet includes a mix of modern, eco-friendly buses equipped with air conditioning and free Wi-Fi on select routes. With regular and reliable service, passengers can count on minimal wait times and convenient access to public transit.

The bus system is designed to serve a diverse population, offering accessibility features like wheelchair ramps and priority seating for passengers with disabilities. Additionally, Valley Metro provides resources such as real-time bus tracking through mobile apps, making it easier for riders to plan their journeys.

The Phoenix Transit Bus is an affordable transportation option and an eco-friendly alternative to driving. By encouraging public transit usage, the bus system reduces traffic congestion and carbon emissions, supporting the city's sustainability goals.

Overall, the Phoenix Transit Bus is a convenient, reliable, and eco-conscious way to explore the vibrant city of Phoenix and its surrounding areas. Whether for daily commuting, leisurely sightseeing, or attending events, the bus system provides a convenient and efficient means of getting around the Valley of the Sun.

Phoenix Dial-A-Ride

This specialized transportation service offered by Valley Metro is designed to cater to the mobility of individuals with disabilities and senior citizens aged 65 and older. This door-to-door, curb-to-curb service provides a lifeline for those with difficulty using traditional public transportation.

Phoenix Dial-A-Ride offers a convenient and personalized transportation solution throughout the Phoenix metropolitan area. Passengers can book rides in advance, ensuring reliable access to medical appointments, grocery stores, community centers, and other essential destinations.

The service is equipped with wheelchair-accessible vehicles and trained drivers sensitive to the unique needs of passengers with disabilities or mobility challenges. Additionally, caregivers or companions can accompany riders to provide further support.

To enhance accessibility and convenience, Phoenix Dial-A-Ride utilizes a user-friendly online booking system and a call center for reservations and inquiries. The service's customer-focused approach ensures that riders receive the assistance they require to travel safely and comfortably.

Phoenix Dial-A-Ride is vital to the city's commitment to fostering inclusivity and independence for all residents. The service promotes equal access to essential services and activities by providing transportation options that accommodate diverse mobility needs.

Phoenix Dial-A-Ride is crucial in enhancing the quality of life for individuals with disabilities and senior citizens, enabling them to remain active, engaged, and connected within their communities. It exemplifies the city's dedication to providing comprehensive and compassionate transportation solutions for all its residents.

Car Rentals - Turo

PRACTICAL INFORMATION & RESOURCES

Using the Turo app to rent a car offers a convenient and innovative way to access a wide range of vehicles for personal transportation. Turo is a peer-to-peer car rental platform that connects car owners with travelers looking to rent a vehicle. The app provides a user-friendly interface, making the rental process simple and efficient.

To begin, users can sign up for a Turo account and browse through a diverse selection of cars available in their location. The app allows renters to filter search results based on vehicle type, features, and price range. Each listing includes detailed information about the car, including photos, specifications, and owner reviews.

Renters can easily book their desired car directly through the app, and owners typically respond promptly to confirm the reservation. Turo offers flexible rental options, allowing users to choose the duration and pick-up location that suits their schedule.

One key advantage of using Turo is the variety of car options available, from budget-friendly economy cars to luxurious and exotic vehicles. Additionally, Turo often provides more competitive rates than traditional car rental companies.

During the rental period, the Turo app offers GPS tracking and digital check-in features, streamlining the pick-up and drop-off process. Renters can also communicate with the car owner through the app for any questions or concerns.

Turo's comprehensive insurance coverage provides car owners and renters peace of mind, ensuring a smooth and worry-free rental experience. Moreover, the app's review system allows users to leave feedback about their rental experience, fostering transparency and accountability within the Turo community.

**If you are staying in any of my rentals, I offer a discount code to select Turo providers in the area.

Door-to-Door Services

Uber/Lyft

Uber or Lyft provides a convenient and reliable alternative to traditional taxis and public transportation. Both ride-hailing platforms utilize user-friendly apps that connect riders with drivers in real time. To use the service, passengers need to download the respective app, create an account, and enter their destination.

Users can view the estimated fare and arrival time when requesting a ride, allowing for better trip planning and budgeting. Payment is automatically processed through the app, eliminating the need for cash transactions.

Uber and Lyft offer a range of vehicle options, from standard economy cars to luxury and SUVs, catering to various preferences and group sizes. Drivers are pre-screened and rated by passengers, ensuring a safe and reliable experience.

The services are available 24/7, making them ideal for late-night or early-morning transportation. Moreover, both platforms offer features like ride-sharing (Uber Pool and Lyft Line) that enable riders to share a car with others going in the same direction, reducing costs and promoting eco-friendliness.

Using Uber or Lyft can be especially beneficial for travelers, providing easy access to local attractions, restaurants, and events without the hassle of renting a car or navigating public transit.

Taxi Cab and Limousine Services

A taxi cab or limousine service offers a classic and reliable way to get around town or attend special events in style. Taxi cabs are less readily available throughout Phoenix and can not be hailed from the street. But they can be booked through a phone call or a website. They provide a quick and convenient mode of transportation, especially for short trips or when public transportation options are limited.

On the other hand, limousine services cater to a more luxurious and upscale experience. They are perfect for special occasions such as weddings, proms, corporate events, or airport transfers. Limousines offer spacious and comfortable interiors, often equipped with amenities like a mini-bar, entertainment systems, and mood lighting.

Both taxi cabs and limousine services typically employ professional and licensed drivers with extensive knowledge of local routes and traffic conditions, ensuring a smooth and efficient ride.

However, it's essential to consider cost, availability, and level of service when choosing between a taxi cab and a limousine. While taxi cabs offer a more economical option for everyday transportation, limousines provide unparalleled luxury and elegance for memorable events.

Ultimately, whether you opt for a taxi cab or a limousine service, both offer the convenience of door-to-door transportation and the advantage of leaving the driving to a professional, allowing you to relax and enjoy the journey.

ACCOMMODATIONS

Corporate or Vacation Rentals

Staying in one of my vacation or corporate rentals in Phoenix offers a unique and personalized experience that allows travelers to feel at home while exploring this vibrant desert city. My rental properties provide all the comforts and amenities of a private residence, creating a sense of space and freedom that traditional hotels may not offer.

With a variety of properties to choose from, travelers can select a home that best suits their needs and preferences. Whether it's a cozy studio apartment for a solo adventurer or a spacious family-friendly home, my rentals cater to different group sizes and lengths of says.

A fully equipped kitchen enables guests to prepare meals and enjoy dining at their own pace. This saves on dining expenses and adds a touch of homey comfort to the vacation experience.

Additionally, the amenities provided in my vacation rentals, such as private pools, outdoor patios, or BBQ grills, allow guests to unwind and relax in privacy after a day of exploring the city's attractions.

Moreover, staying in one of my rentals provides an opportunity to live like a local, immersing oneself in the neighborhood and community. Guests can discover hidden gems and experience the city from a different perspective, away from the tourist crowds. Especially since you're staying in a home offered by the author of this book!

The personalized attention and care I provide as a host ensures that guests have a memorable and enjoyable stay. From quick responses to inquiries and local tips to ensuring the property is well-maintained and clean, your commitment to hospitality leaves a positive impression on guests.

**Be sure to visit SunshineHillProperties.com for contact information and book a stay. If one of my properties doesn't fit your needs, I can help place you into another home that does.*

Hotels

Phoenix offers a variety of hotels with water slides, making it an ideal destination for families and water enthusiasts. These hotels provide a perfect blend of relaxation and excitement for guests of all ages.

These water slide hotels often feature impressive water parks with thrilling slides, lazy rivers, splash pads, and pools, creating a fun-filled oasis in the desert heat. Families can spend hours enjoying the water attractions, making cherished memories together.

In addition to water slides, these hotels typically offer other family-friendly amenities such as kids' clubs, game rooms, and family-friendly dining options. Adults can also enjoy relaxing poolside with a refreshing drink from the pool bar.

Some hotels with water slides are conveniently near popular attractions, shopping centers, and dining options, allowing guests to explore the best of Phoenix during their stay.

RV Parks

Phoenix is a popular destination for RV enthusiasts, and the city offers a range of well-equipped and comfortable RV parks to accommodate travelers. These RV parks provide a convenient and enjoyable stay while exploring the natural beauty and attractions of the Phoenix area.

Most RV parks in Phoenix offer spacious and level sites with full hookups, including water, electricity, and sewer connections, ensuring a comfortable stay for all RVs. Some parks also provide additional amenities such as cable TV, Wi-Fi, laundry facilities, and well-maintained restrooms and showers.

In addition to the essential amenities, many RV parks boast recreational facilities such as swimming pools, hot tubs, fitness centers, and outdoor recreation areas, creating a welcoming environment for guests to relax and socialize.

The location of these RV parks is another major draw, with many situated near popular attractions like hiking trails, golf courses, and cultural landmarks. Some parks even offer shuttle services to nearby attractions, eliminating the need to drive their RVs.

Community and camaraderie among fellow RVers is a highlight of staying at these parks. Many RV parks organize social events, potlucks, and group activities, providing opportunities for guests to connect and make new friends.

Whether it's a short stay or an extended vacation, RV parks in Phoenix offer a home-away-from-home experience for travelers seeking to immerse themselves in this desert city's beauty and outdoor adventures. The well-maintained facilities, friendly atmosphere, and convenient location make Phoenix's RV parks an excellent choice for an enjoyable and memorable RVing experience in Arizona.

SAFETY TIPS

When traveling to Phoenix, it's essential to prioritize safety for a smooth and enjoyable trip. Here are some safety tips to keep in mind:

1. Stay Hydrated: Phoenix has a desert climate with scorching temperatures, especially in the summer. Always carry a water bottle and stay hydrated, especially when exploring outdoor attractions.
2. Sun Protection: Wear sunscreen, sunglasses, and a wide-brimmed

hat to protect yourself from the intense Arizona sun. Limit outdoor activities during peak heat hours (usually between 10 am and 4 pm).
3. Watch for Wildlife: Arizona is home to various wildlife, including snakes and scorpions. Be cautious when hiking, and always stay on marked trails.
4. Be Cautious with Water Activities: If enjoying water sports or activities in natural bodies of water, be aware of hazards like strong currents or flash floods.
5. Secure Valuables: Petty theft can occur in tourist areas. Keep your belongings secure, and avoid leaving valuables in your car or unattended.
6. Be Mindful of Heat Exhaustion: Watch for signs of heat exhaustion, such as dizziness, rapid heartbeat, or nausea. Seek shade and drink water if you start feeling unwell.
7. Plan for Monsoons: Monsoon season (July to September) can bring heavy rains and sudden storms. Be prepared for weather changes and avoid low-lying areas during heavy rainfall.
8. Follow Traffic Laws: Phoenix has busy roads, so obey traffic laws and avoid distractions.
9. Know Emergency Numbers: Familiarize yourself with local emergency contact numbers, including police, fire, and medical services.
10. Respect Wildlife and Nature: Avoid disturbing or feeding wildlife, as it can harm them and potentially harm you.
11. Use Reputable Transportation: When using ride-sharing services, verify the driver's information and ensure you're using a reputable company.
12. Carry Identification: Always carry identification and let someone know your itinerary if exploring remote areas.
13. Research Trail Conditions: Check for trail conditions and weather updates before hiking or exploring natural areas.
14. Be Water-Wise: If visiting the Salt River or other water recreation spots, practice water safety and wear appropriate gear.
15. Stay Informed: Stay updated on weather forecasts, local news, and safety advisories during your visit.

PRACTICAL INFORMATION & RESOURCES

By following these tips, you can enjoy your time in Phoenix, AZ, with peace of mind and make the most of your experience in this vibrant desert city.

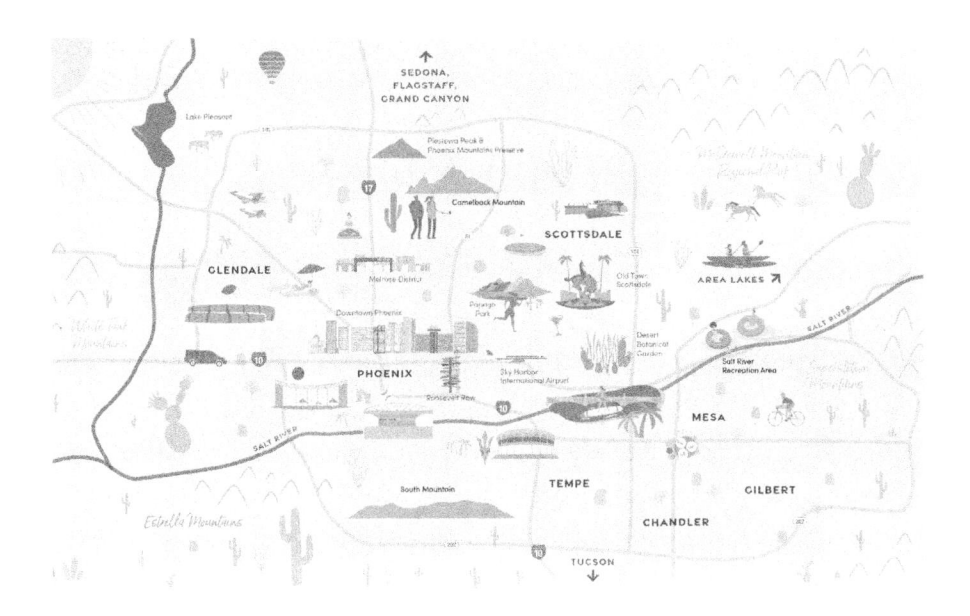

9

Thank You!

Wow, this guide was a lot longer than I anticipated. There's so much fun stuff to do that I struggled to decide what to keep in the pages and what to leave out. I will need to update this in a few years to add some new attractions because Phoenix is growing like wildfire.

The following pages are prompted with sections in the book. Use them to journal about your experiences in and around Phoenix! I hope you come to love this wonderful desert city as much as I have.

I would love to hear how you enjoyed this book, so leave me a **_5-star review on Amazon!_** It helps others find this book so they can create memories of their own.

As a reminder, I'm a Realtor here in Phoenix, and I'm happy to help you find a corporate/vacation rental in one of my properties for your trip. Also, Phoenix is one of the fastest-growing cities in America because job growth is off the charts. If you fall in love with Phoenix during your stay and want a home here, I'd love to assist. Whether it becomes your primary residence or a second home, I can help you find the property that best fits your needs. Creating passive income by investing in properties that can be used as

THANK YOU!

corporate or vacation rentals is an exciting choice for some. I can help you strategize a plan to make that vision a reality.

Thank you for your purchase of this book. I look forward to reading your review on Amazon!

10

Journal Prompts

JOURNAL PROMPTS

Museums

DATE:

TRAVEL TO PHOENIX, ARIZONA

Museums

DATE:

JOURNAL PROMPTS

DATE: *Museums*

TRAVEL TO PHOENIX, ARIZONA

Theaters

DATE:

JOURNAL PROMPTS

Theaters

DATE:

TRAVEL TO PHOENIX, ARIZONA

Theaters

DATE:

JOURNAL PROMPTS

Old Town Scottsdale

DATE:

Old Town Scottsdale

DATE:

JOURNAL PROMPTS

Old Town Scottsdale

DATE:

TRAVEL TO PHOENIX, ARIZONA

Roosevelt Row

DATE:

JOURNAL PROMPTS

Roosevelt Row

DATE:

TRAVEL TO PHOENIX, ARIZONA

Roosevelt Row

DATE:

JOURNAL PROMPTS

DATE: *Hiking*

SUNSHINE HILL
PROPERTIES

TRAVEL TO PHOENIX, ARIZONA

DATE: *Hiking*

SUNSHINE HILL
PROPERTIES

JOURNAL PROMPTS

DATE: *Hiking*

TRAVEL TO PHOENIX, ARIZONA

Lakes

DATE:

JOURNAL PROMPTS

Lakes

DATE:

TRAVEL TO PHOENIX, ARIZONA

Lakes

DATE:

JOURNAL PROMPTS

Camping

DATE:

TRAVEL TO PHOENIX, ARIZONA

Camping

DATE:

JOURNAL PROMPTS

Camping

DATE:

TRAVEL TO PHOENIX, ARIZONA

Night Life

DATE:

JOURNAL PROMPTS

DATE: *Night Life*

TRAVEL TO PHOENIX, ARIZONA

DATE: *Night Life*

JOURNAL PROMPTS

DATE: Aquariums & Zoos

TRAVEL TO PHOENIX, ARIZONA

DATE: Aquariums & Zoos

JOURNAL PROMPTS

DATE: *Aquariums & Zoos*

TRAVEL TO PHOENIX, ARIZONA

DATE: *Fun with the Kids*

JOURNAL PROMPTS

DATE: Fun with the Kids

TRAVEL TO PHOENIX, ARIZONA

DATE: Fun with the Kids

JOURNAL PROMPTS

Theme & Water Parks

DATE:

TRAVEL TO PHOENIX, ARIZONA

Theme & Water Parks

DATE:

JOURNAL PROMPTS

Theme & Water Parks

DATE:

TRAVEL TO PHOENIX, ARIZONA

Botanical Gardens

DATE:

JOURNAL PROMPTS

Botanical Gardens

DATE:

TRAVEL TO PHOENIX, ARIZONA

Botanical Gardens

DATE:

JOURNAL PROMPTS

Adventuring

DATE:

TRAVEL TO PHOENIX, ARIZONA

Adventuring

DATE:

JOURNAL PROMPTS

Adventuring

DATE:

TRAVEL TO PHOENIX, ARIZONA

Shopping

DATE:

JOURNAL PROMPTS

Shopping

DATE:

TRAVEL TO PHOENIX, ARIZONA

Shopping

DATE:

JOURNAL PROMPTS

Spa Day

DATE:

TRAVEL TO PHOENIX, ARIZONA

Spa Day

DATE:

JOURNAL PROMPTS

Spa Day

DATE:

TRAVEL TO PHOENIX, ARIZONA

Fitness

DATE:

JOURNAL PROMPTS

Fitness

DATE:

TRAVEL TO PHOENIX, ARIZONA

Fitness

DATE:

JOURNAL PROMPTS

DATE: The Footprint Center

TRAVEL TO PHOENIX, ARIZONA

State Farm Stadium

DATE:

JOURNAL PROMPTS

DATE: *Chase Field*

TRAVEL TO PHOENIX, ARIZONA

DATE: *Spring Training*

JOURNAL PROMPTS

DATE: *Arizona Coyotes*

TRAVEL TO PHOENIX, ARIZONA

DATE: WM Phoenix Open

JOURNAL PROMPTS

Golfing

DATE:

TRAVEL TO PHOENIX, ARIZONA

DATE: *Casinos*

JOURNAL PROMPTS

Arizona State University

DATE:

TRAVEL TO PHOENIX, ARIZONA

DATE: *Casual Dinner*

JOURNAL PROMPTS

DATE: Casual Dinner

TRAVEL TO PHOENIX, ARIZONA

DATE: *Casual Dinner*

JOURNAL PROMPTS

Cultural Menu

DATE:

TRAVEL TO PHOENIX, ARIZONA

Cultural Menu

DATE:

JOURNAL PROMPTS

Cultural Menu

DATE:

TRAVEL TO PHOENIX, ARIZONA

DATE: *Farm to Table*

JOURNAL PROMPTS

DATE: Farm to Table

TRAVEL TO PHOENIX, ARIZONA

DATE: Farm to Table

JOURNAL PROMPTS

Fine Dining

DATE:

TRAVEL TO PHOENIX, ARIZONA

Fine Dining

DATE:

JOURNAL PROMPTS

Fine Dining

DATE:

Craft Beer & Local Wine

DATE:

JOURNAL PROMPTS

Craft Beer & Local Wine

DATE:

TRAVEL TO PHOENIX, ARIZONA

Craft Beer & Local Wine

DATE:

JOURNAL PROMPTS

DATE: **Food Trucks**

TRAVEL TO PHOENIX, ARIZONA

DATE: **Food Trucks**

JOURNAL PROMPTS

DATE: **Food Trucks**

TRAVEL TO PHOENIX, ARIZONA

DATE: With the Kids

JOURNAL PROMPTS

DATE: *With the Kids*

TRAVEL TO PHOENIX, ARIZONA

DATE: *With the Kids*

JOURNAL PROMPTS

DATE: Patios & Rooftops

TRAVEL TO PHOENIX, ARIZONA

DATE: *Patios & Rooftops*

JOURNAL PROMPTS

DATE: Patios & Rooftops

Desserts & Bakeries

DATE:

Desserts & Bakeries

DATE:

TRAVEL TO PHOENIX, ARIZONA

Desserts & Bakeries

DATE:

JOURNAL PROMPTS

Coffee Shops

DATE:

TRAVEL TO PHOENIX, ARIZONA

Coffee Shops

DATE:

JOURNAL PROMPTS

Coffee Shops

DATE:

TRAVEL TO PHOENIX, ARIZONA

DATE: Sedona, AZ

JOURNAL PROMPTS

DATE: Sedona, AZ

TRAVEL TO PHOENIX, ARIZONA

DATE: Sedona, AZ

JOURNAL PROMPTS

Jerome, AZ

DATE:

Jerome, AZ

DATE:

JOURNAL PROMPTS

Jerome, AZ

DATE:

TRAVEL TO PHOENIX, ARIZONA

DATE: **Bisbee, AZ**

JOURNAL PROMPTS

DATE: Bisbee, AZ

TRAVEL TO PHOENIX, ARIZONA

DATE: Bisbee, AZ

JOURNAL PROMPTS

DATE: Flagstaff, AZ

TRAVEL TO PHOENIX, ARIZONA

DATE: Flagstaff, AZ

JOURNAL PROMPTS

DATE: Flagstaff, AZ

TRAVEL TO PHOENIX, ARIZONA

DATE: *The Grand Canyon*

JOURNAL PROMPTS

DATE: The Grand Canyon

TRAVEL TO PHOENIX, ARIZONA

DATE: The Grand Canyon

JOURNAL PROMPTS

DATE: Tombstone, AZ

TRAVEL TO PHOENIX, ARIZONA

DATE: Tombstone, AZ

JOURNAL PROMPTS

DATE: Tombstone, AZ

TRAVEL TO PHOENIX, ARIZONA

DATE: Rocky Point, Mexico

JOURNAL PROMPTS

DATE: Rocky Point, Mexico

TRAVEL TO PHOENIX, ARIZONA

DATE: Rocky Point, Mexico

About the Author

Ashley Atwood, born and raised in Bryan, TX, was always a bit of a wanderlust. With ambitions to be a professional performer in Dance and Acting, she moved to New York City to launch her career. There she studied with top choreographers at Steps on Broadway and eventually migrated to the west coast in Los Angeles, CA. She quickly began working in film and television while studying Acting at Playhouse West with Robert Carnegie and Holly Gagnier. Her film career blossomed, and she eventually earned an Academy of Television Arts and Sciences (Emmy) Nomination for her work in Rekindling Christmas, a film she produced and shot back in her hometown of Bryan, TX! During the pandemic, Ashley decided to switch things up and dive into other passions of hers, Family & Real Estate. She moved to Phoenix with her husband and earned her Arizona Department of Real Estate License. Now, she helps others buy and sell real estate, invests in her portfolio of vacation and corporate rentals, and loves spending time with her husband and two sons.

You can connect with me on:

- https://www.sunshinehillproperties.com
- https://facebook.com/sunshinehillproperties
- https://www.instagram.com/sunshinehill_properties

Printed in Great Britain
by Amazon